THE SECRET IS OUT

William Stanek is the artist behind the scenes at World Galleries, and the fiction author Robert Stanek.

BW Fall Arrives at Multnomah Falls in Canvas Print with Floating Frame

Find his art at 360 Studios

360studios.pictorem.com

williamrstanek.com

Note on Listening to Reader Feedback

At **Living Well Pathways**, our journey has always been about creating meaningful, impactful tools for personal growth. Over time, we've had the privilege of engaging with our readers—hearing your stories, learning from your insights, and understanding what truly resonates.

Your feedback has been the catalyst for this completely revised and refreshed approach. We've embraced your input, addressing the challenges you face, deepening the content, and expanding the tools to make this series even more actionable and relatable.

This updated version reflects not just our vision but also your voices. It's a testament to the power of collaboration and the shared journey toward authenticity, resilience, and purpose. Thank you for guiding us and being part of the *Living Well Pathways* evolution. Together, we're shaping a path that's as dynamic and impactful as the lives we aspire to lead.

Living Well Pathways Series Overview

Living Well Pathways represents a groundbreaking departure from traditional self-help literature. This series redefines personal development by embracing life's chaos, celebrating individuality, and providing actionable tools to navigate the complexities of modern existence. Here's what sets it apart:

Why Living Well Pathways Stands Out:

- **Authentic, No-Nonsense Approach:** Unlike traditional self-help narratives that focus on overly simplified solutions or rigid frameworks, Living Well Pathways embraces the messiness of life. It encourages readers to confront challenges directly, using chaos as a catalyst for growth instead of avoiding or masking it.
- **Active Participation Over Passive Reflection:** Where books like The Secret emphasize visualization and positivity, this series advocates for intentional action. It empowers readers to actively shape their lives, fostering resilience and self-discovery by engaging fully with life's complexities.
- **Dynamic and Evolving Purpose:** Purpose isn't static—it's a journey. Rather than offering one-size-fits-all solutions, Living Well Pathways helps readers uncover a purpose that evolves alongside their experiences, embracing uncertainty and growth.
- **Balancing Realism with Optimism:** While many personal development books focus on relentless positivity or unyielding faith, this series blends optimism with realism. It acknowledges that life includes both triumphs and struggles, teaching readers to navigate both with grace and grit.
- **Celebration of Individuality:** Rather than adhering to societal norms or traditional definitions of success, Living Well Pathways encourages readers to embrace their unique voices and chart paths that align with their core values.

- **Focus on Action and Impact:** Beyond self-reflection, this series emphasizes taking meaningful action. Readers are guided to create lasting impacts in their personal lives and communities, reinforcing that authentic living extends beyond the self.

The Living Well Pathways Series

Book 1: Chisel Your Path – Carving Authenticity and Purpose in the Chaos of Life

- **Focus:** Learn how to shape your life intentionally by cutting through distractions and uncovering your authentic self.
- **Key Themes:** Prioritization, authenticity, and navigating chaos with purpose.
- **Unique Value:** Offers practical, actionable tools to actively shape your journey, rather than merely reflecting on it.

Book 2: Harmony in the Chaos – Cultivating Balance and Resonance in Life's Symphony

- **Focus:** Achieve harmony in life's multifaceted challenges, from relationships to personal growth.
- **Key Themes:** Balancing priorities, embracing life's diversity, and cultivating meaningful connections.
- **Unique Value:** Helps readers manage life's competing demands with nuance, fostering a sense of deep balance and connection.

Book 3: Orchestrating Impact – Conducting Life's Symphony with Purpose and Resilience

- **Focus:** Discover how to lead with purpose and build resilience to make a meaningful impact in the world.
- **Key Themes:** Leadership, lasting impact, and thriving through challenges.
- **Unique Value:** Combines inspirational storytelling with strategies to create personal and societal transformation.

Single Volume: Embrace Chaos, Find Purpose
- **Comprehensive Edition:** Combines all three books, creating a cohesive guide to self-discovery, balance, and impact.
- **Exclusive Feature:** Includes The Resilient Growth Self-Assessment Tool, a $65 value, integrated into an interactive app for personalized development insights.

Who is Living Well Pathways For?

- •Those seeking authentic personal growth without the sugarcoating.
- •Individuals striving to embrace life's unpredictability and transform chaos into opportunity.
- •Readers ready to align their actions with their core values and create meaningful, lasting impact.
- •Anyone looking for practical tools and strategies to foster resilience, purpose, and balance.

Why Choose Living Well Pathways?

Living Well Pathways challenges you to reject superficial self-help clichés. It's an invitation to embrace your individuality, honor your struggles, and craft a life of authenticity and purpose. This series isn't just a guide—it's a movement toward living with intention and creating ripples of impact in the world.

Start your journey today, and discover what it means to truly live well amidst life's chaos.

Dear Seekers of Depth, Authenticity, and Meaning

In the vast, ever-shifting sea of personal growth, there lies a tapestry woven from the threads of experience, courage, and an unwavering commitment to living a life that truly resonates. This tapestry is not merely a collection of thoughts or a set of lessons—it's an offering, a guide, and an invitation to embark on a journey toward an existence that feels fully and genuinely lived.

As we explore what it means to care about what truly matters, to navigate the tangled web of priorities, and to shape our lives with intention, remember that these concepts are interconnected. They form a cohesive foundation upon which a fulfilling life is built. This book is more than just a map for personal growth; it's the essence of years spent giving careful thought, making mistakes, and savoring moments of unapologetic joy.

This isn't a typical self-help book. It's a counterpoint to the status quo, a celebration of the beautifully imperfect journey toward authenticity, and a guide for navigating the complexities of our world with resilience, flair, and an unwavering commitment to meaningful growth.

The journey of personal evolution isn't only about triumphs—it's also about responsibility. With each step toward self-discovery comes the profound duty to shape our own narrative. My own path has been one of transformation, where I've found strength in introspection and growth amid challenges. Standing at the crossroads of chaos, authenticity, and purpose, I've gathered insights that have deeply influenced my approach to living a life that matters.

Throughout my journey, I've been privileged to witness and engage in pivotal moments of personal and collective transformation—from the liberating act of saying "no" to what no longer serves us, to the joyful embrace of unapologetic authenticity. These experiences have underscored the power of personal growth, especially in times of adversity, and have reinforced my belief that real transformation transcends fleeting trends. True growth demands the courage to explore, the resilience to challenge norms, and the adaptability to navigate life's complexities.

As we embark on this journey together, I invite you to challenge conventional expectations, to venture into the uncharted territories of your true self, and to embrace the creativity and courage inherent in living authentically. May these pages serve as a guide for your own path, one that leads you to a life filled with purpose, passion, and genuine joy.

With warmest regards and encouragement, *William R. Stanek*

Orchestrating Impact: Conducting Life's Symphony with Purpose and Resilience

Living Well Pathways, Book 3

William R. Stanek
Author & Series Creator

Orchestrating Impact: Conducting Life's Symphony with Purpose and Resilience

Living Well Pathways, Book 3

Published by Stanek & Associates
in conjunction with
Big Blue Sky Press for Business
www.williamrstanek.com.

2nd Edition Copyright © 2026 William R. Stanek. Seattle, Washington. All rights reserved. Photographs of the author are © HC Stanek. Fine-art photographs and illustrations are © William R. Stanek and were created by the author.

No part of this book may be reproduced, stored in a retrieval system or transmitted in any form or by any means, electronic, mechanical, photocopying, recording, scanning or otherwise, except as permitted by Sections 107 or 108 of the 1976 United States Copyright Act, without the prior written permission of the publisher Requests to the publisher for permission should be sent to the address listed previously.

Stanek & Associates is a trademark of Stanek & Associates and/or its affiliates. All other marks are the property of their respective owners. No association with any real company, organization, person or other named element is intended or should be inferred through use of company names, web site addresses or screens.

This book expresses the views and opinions of the author. The information contained in this book is provided without any express, statutory or implied warranties.

LIMIT OF LIABILITY/DISCLAIMER OF WARRANTY: THE PUBLISHER AND THE AUTHOR MAKE NO REPRESENTATIONS OR WARRANTIES WITH RESPECT TO THE ACCURACY OR COMPLETENESS OF THE CONTENTS OF THIS WORK AND SPECIFICALLY DISCLAIM ALL WARRANTIES, INCLUDING WITHOUT LIMITATION WARRANTIES OF FITNESS FOR A PARTICULAR PURPOSE. NO WARRANTY MAY BE CREATED OR EXTENDD BY SALES OR PROMOTIONAL MATERIALS. THE ADVICE AND DISCUSSION IN THIS BOOK MAY NOT BE SUITABLE FOR EVERY SITUATION. THIS WORK IS SOLD WITH THE UNDERSTANDING THTAT THE PUBLISHER IS NOT ENGAGED IN RENDERING PROFESSIONAL SERVICES AND THAT SHOULD PROFESSIONAL ASSISTANCE BE REQUIRED THE SERVICES OF A COMPETENT PROFESSIONAL SHOULD BE SOUGHT. NEITHER THE PUBLISHERS, AUTHORS, RESELLERS NOR DISTRIBUTORS SHALL

BE HELD LIABLE FOR ANY DAMAGES CAUSED OR ALLEGED TO BE CAUSE EITHER DIRECTLY OR INDIRECTLY HEREFROM. THE REFERENCE OF AN ORGANIZATION OR WEBSITE AS A SOURCE OF FURTHER INFORMATION DOES NOT MEAN THAT THE PUBLISHER OR THE AUTHOR ENDORSES THE INFORMATION THE ORGANIZATION OR WEBSITE MAY PROVIDE OR THE RECOMMENDATIONS IT MAY MAKE. FURTHER, READERS SHOULD BE AWARE THAT WEBSITES LISTED IN THIS BOOK MAY NOT BE AVAILABLE OR MAY HAVE CHANGED SINCE THIS WORK WAS WRITTEN.

Stanek & Associates publishes in a variety of formats, including print, electronic and by print-on-demand. Some materials included with standard print editions may not be included in electronic or print-on-demand editions or vice versa.

Country of First Publication: United States of America.

Cover Design: Creative Designs Ltd.
Editorial Development: Andover Publishing Solutions
Content & Technical Review: L & L Technical Content Services

You can provide feedback related to this book by emailing the author at williamstanek @ aol.com. Please use the <u>name of the book</u> as the subject line.

2nd Edition. Version: 2.1.5.1c

> **Note** I may periodically update this text and the edition and version number shown previously will let you know which version you are working with. If there's a specific feature you'd like me to write about, message me on Facebook (http://facebook.com/williamstanekauthor). Please keep in mind readership of this book determines how much time I can dedicate to it.

Table of Contents

Note on Listening to Reader Feedback 2
Living Well Pathways Series Overview 3
Dear Seekers of Depth, Authenticity, and Meaning 6
Table of Contents 13
To the Seekers of Authenticity, the Challengers of Convention, and the Keepers of Unconventional Wisdom, ... 17
6-Week Action Plan for Orchestrating Impact: Conducting Life's Symphony with Purpose and Resilience 21
The Symphony Within 23
Week 1 27
Week 1 Action Plan: Diving Deep into Your Symphony 28
The Circus Tent 31
The Messy Threads That Weave Our Lives 36
The Echo Chamber 41
Not Your Grandma's Etiquette Class 46
The Cookie-Cutter Catastrophe 51
Week 2 57
Week 2 Action Plan: Cultivating Connections and Creative Chaos 58
The Art of Creative Chaos 61
The Jungle of Human Connection 69
The Unhealthy Connections 74

The Emotional Stock Exchange..................................82
Forging Your Own Path..................................88
The Drumbeat You Can't Ignore..................................96
Week 3 101
Week 3 Action Plan: Deepening Authenticity and Embracing the Uncharted 102
Where Every Voice is Heard 105
That Dissonant Note 110
Investing in Vintage Experiences..................................117
Life Without Rose-Tinted Glasses..................................121
Blind to the Gems 126
No Rehearsed Speeches 131
Week 4 135
Week 4 Action Plan: Embracing Your Unique Journey and Mastering Balance 136
The Humble Reminder 140
It Glitters Like the Sun 144
Courageous Self-Expression..................................149
The Wild, Unrestrained Extravaganza of Life..................................154
Not Your Grandma's Library 158
The Oracle Within 162
Week 5 167
Week 5 Action Plan: Deepening Resonance and Strengthening Your Compass 168
The Red Button Syndrome 172
The Unsung Hero of Life..................................176
The Intent Matters..................................181
The Symphony of Serendipity..................................187
It's Not About Likes and Emojis..................................192

Storms Don't Weaken Your Lighthouse	197
Week 6	203
Week 6 Action Plan: Navigating Uncharted Waters	204
Master that Compass Already!	207
The Occasional Cosmic Curveball	213
The Map to Liberation	218
Back to the Garden	222
Unlike Jellyfish Take Aim	227
Life's Balancing Act	231
Afterword for the Book	243
About the Author: William R. Stanek	245

To the Seekers of Authenticity, the Challengers of Convention, and the Keepers of Unconventional Wisdom,

The journey of exploring meaningful growth and understanding what truly matters has been profound—a journey shaped by the twists, turns, and insights gained from years of navigating the unpredictable landscape of life. I want to express my deepest gratitude to those who have been part of this path with me. You are the ones who truly understand the challenges, the revisions, and the years that went into bringing this book to life.

First, my heartfelt thanks to those who have dared to question the norms—from the visionaries sharing ideas in coffee shops to the dedicated souls crafting their own paths. Your confidence in my work and your willingness to entrust me with unraveling life's complexities have been both humbling and inspiring. This book is a tribute to your courage and indomitable spirit.

To the many friends and mentors with whom I've shared this dynamic journey, thank you. Each knowing smile, every shared "What are we doing here?" moment, has contributed to the insights and perspectives that fill these pages. Your openness to embracing life's uncertainties, your defiance of convention, and your passion for innovation have all been sources of inspiration.

To my collaborators and confidants, past and present—thank you for being partners in this creative process. Your wisdom, often shared over long conversations and caffeine-fueled brainstorms, has added depth to this work. Together, we have challenged conventions, given shape to new ideas, and explored concepts that resist being confined.

Special thanks go to those who offered invaluable feedback, contributed fresh perspectives, and engaged in vibrant discussions that helped shape this book. Your unconventional ideas and commitment to thoughtful exploration are woven into every chapter. This work is as much yours as it is mine.

This book is a journey through the shared wisdom of those who have left their mark on the world—proof that real leadership is about audacious actions and meaningful impact rather than titles. It's a tribute to those who have shown that each of us holds the potential to lead with purpose, with empathy, and with a vision for positive change.

Finally, to my family—thank you for your unwavering support and patience. Your belief in me and in the purpose behind this book has been the fuel that sustained me through the process. This book carries the mark of your steadfast encouragement as much as it does my own journey.

With deepest gratitude and respect,

William R. Stanek

6-Week Action Plan for Orchestrating Impact: Conducting Life's Symphony with Purpose and Resilience

Congratulations on reaching the crescendo of "Orchestrating Impact," the concluding volume of "Embrace Chaos, Find Purpose." This journey is an exploration into how you can lead with purpose, build resilience against life's adversities, and create a lasting impact in your world. The chapters serve as individual notes in the grand symphony of your life, teaching you to embrace leadership, impact, resilience, and the relentless pursuit of purpose.

As you stand on the threshold of this journey's end, it's time to translate the symphony of insights into a concerto of action. Each chapter is crafted for quick engagement, but hold back from consuming the entire book in one session or even within a brief week. Dedicate a whole day to delve into each chapter, deeply connecting with the insights and reflections it provides. Embrace the content thoroughly, become intimately familiar with its messages, and let the seeds of transformation take root and grow within you. This journey is more than just reading; it's an invitation to sync with your inner rebel, offering a detailed path to unleash the full orchestra of your capabilities, especially as you navigate life's balancing act.

Revisiting the chapters will allow you to deepen your connection with each theme, uncovering new nuances and empowering you to fine-tune your approach to life's complex score. To bridge the gap between reflection and action, we've interwoven a six-week action plan throughout the text. This integrated approach, distinct from the standalone action plans in the earlier books, is designed to facilitate a smoother assimilation of strategies, practices, and insights, ensuring the harmony of your actions aligns with the melody of your aspirations. Consider this plan as your conductor's baton, guiding you towards a life marked by meaningful impact and resonant fulfillment.

The Symphony Within

In the depths of your being lies a symphony—a masterful composition of courage, resilience, and authenticity. In a world drowning in noise and chaos, it is here, within your inner orchestra, that you find the most profound and personal melody. This chapter invites you to take up the conductor's baton and craft a symphony that is uniquely, unapologetically yours.

Too often, life feels like an overwhelming orchestra, its instruments clamoring with external expectations. Societal norms blare like brass horns; family pressures tap out unrelenting percussion; comparison hums a ceaseless, insidious tune. Yet, amid this cacophony, you hold the power to quiet the external noise and attune yourself to the melody within. The first step? Tune out the noise, reclaim the silence, and listen for the notes that have always been waiting for you.

Picture your inner symphony as an overture of self-discovery. It isn't about mastering someone else's sheet music but about honoring your unique composition. Each instrument within your orchestra represents a distinct facet of your identity—qualities and strengths waiting to be brought to life. To fully embrace this melody, you must shed the expectations of conformity and embrace the authenticity of your own sound.

Imagine this: the soaring crescendo of unapologetic authenticity reverberating through the halls of your life. Authenticity is not just about "being yourself"; it is a bold, deliberate declaration of your essence. Let each note resonate with the truth of who you are and what you stand for. In this symphony, there is no room for half-hearted playing. You are the composer, the conductor, and the audience.

Every great symphony relies on its instruments. In the orchestra of your life, each section embodies an essential part of your journey:

- **The Percussion of Courage:** Life often demands bold, decisive action. Each courageous choice is a beat that propels you forward. This percussion is not about blindly forging ahead; it is about deliberate, fearless steps in alignment with your core values.
- **The Strings of Resilience:** Like strings, your resilience is plucked by challenges and adversity, yet it vibrates with enduring strength. These strings transform discord into harmony, reminding you that life's hardships are not interruptions but essential movements in your melody.
- **The Brass of Boldness:** The brass section declares your presence. Trumpets announce your worth, while trombones amplify your convictions. Boldness is not arrogance; it is the unapologetic affirmation of your right to exist and thrive.
- **The Woodwinds of Adaptability:** Graceful and flowing, the woodwinds embody your ability to bend without breaking. They remind you that flexibility is not weakness but the graceful ability to adapt without losing your essence.
- **The Choir of Self-Compassion:** The human voice is the heart of any symphony. Let your inner choir sing not with self-criticism but with compassion. Each note acknowledges your imperfections and strengths, creating a rich and honest harmony.

Amid the crescendos and cadences of life, silence emerges as the unsung hero. Silence is not an absence of sound but a deliberate pause, a moment to reflect, regroup, and realign. These interludes are where the true work of self-discovery begins.

- **Silence as Reflection:** Like the rests in a musical score, moments of silence provide balance and meaning to your melody. In these spaces, you confront your fears, celebrate your joys, and explore the nuances of your identity.
- **Silence as Growth:** Personal growth often occurs in the stillness between actions. In quiet moments, lessons take root, and new possibilities emerge.
- **Silence as Clarity:** Just as a bell's chime is most profound in stillness, the truth of your being resonates most clearly in silence. These pauses allow your inner voice to rise above the noise, guiding you with wisdom and intuition.

As the conductor of your life, you wield the baton of personal power. This role is not about controlling every note but about directing the flow of your symphony with intention. Boundaries serve as your sheet music, ensuring that the instruments of your life play in harmony rather than discord. Spontaneity, like a jazz improvisation, invites you to embrace the unexpected with creativity and joy.

Your symphony is a celebration of individuality. Each instrument, note, and rest contributes to a composition that is uniquely yours. The piano sonata of your life reflects the interplay of your passions, strengths, and vulnerabilities. Let your fingers dance across the keys, unafraid of the occasional wrong note. Every sound, even discord, has its place in the masterpiece.

A symphony is never truly solo. While your individual melody is vital, the harmonies created through connection with others enrich the experience. Shared experiences, mutual respect, and collaborative efforts amplify the beauty of your life's composition.

The symphony within is a dynamic, ever-evolving masterpiece. With each new experience, your composition grows richer and more complex. Lifelong learning ensures that your melody remains vibrant, your harmony enriched by the wisdom gained through trials and triumphs alike.

Key Takeaways

- **Embrace Authenticity:** Your symphony is yours alone to compose. Let each note reflect your truth.
- **Silence as Strength:** Use moments of quiet reflection to find clarity, growth, and purpose.
- **Courage and Resilience:** Bold decisions and the ability to endure hardships form the backbone of your melody.
- **Connection and Harmony:** Balance individuality with the enriching harmonies of shared experiences.
- **Eternal Evolution:** Your symphony is never complete. Lifelong learning ensures its vibrancy and depth.

Let this chapter be your invitation to embrace the extraordinary music of your existence. Take up the baton, silence the noise, and compose a symphony that resonates with authenticity, passion, and purpose. The world doesn't need another copy; it needs your masterpiece. Play on.

Week 1

Week 1 Action Plan: Diving Deep into Your Symphony

This leg of your journey has been about recognizing your inner strength, leading with resilience, and making a meaningful impact. It's time to reflect, act, and amplify the impact you wish to create in the world and within yourself.

Day 1: Reflection on "The Symphony Within"

- **Activity:** Spend 20 minutes in solitude reflecting on your inner strengths and weaknesses. Write down what makes your personal symphony unique. Identify which parts of your life you're leading with purpose and where you might be merely following the crowd.
- **Reflection:** How does your inner symphony guide your daily actions?

Day 2: "The Circus Tent" Exploration

- **Activity:** Visualize your life as a circus. Identify the acts (areas of your life) that are thrilling and those that feel like they're underperforming. Sketch or write down ideas on how to bring more balance and excitement to your personal circus.
- **Reflection:** Which act of your life's circus are you most proud of, and why?

Day 3: Weaving "The Messy Threads That Weave Our Lives"
- **Activity:** List the top 5 relationships in your life. Next to each, note how these relationships contribute to your tapestry and one action you can take to strengthen each thread.
- **Reflection:** How do these relationships influence your resilience and impact?

Day 4: Entering "The Echo Chamber"
- **Activity:** Identify a recent decision influenced by external expectations rather than your own desires. Reevaluate this decision from your authentic perspective and consider any adjustments you'd like to make.
- **Reflection:** How often do you find yourself influenced by the echo chamber, and what can you do to resist its pull?

Day 5: "Not Your Grandma's Etiquette Class" - Defining Your Values
- **Activity:** Create a personal code of values that you want to live by. Consider what is non-negotiable for you and what guides your decisions.
- **Reflection:** How do these values align with the impact you wish to create?

Day 6: "The Cookie-Cutter Catastrophe" - Embracing Individuality
- **Activity:** Reflect on areas of your life where you feel you're conforming to societal norms at the expense of your individuality. Plan one action you can take to break free from one of these "cookie-cutter" molds.
- **Reflection:** How does conforming or not conforming affect your mental and emotional energy?

Day 7: Weekly Synthesis
- **Activity:** Review your reflections and activities from the week. Combine them into a personal manifesto for leading a life of

purpose and resilience. Share this manifesto with someone you trust, or keep it as a personal reminder.
- **Reflection:** Reflect on how this week's activities have shifted your perspective on making an impact and leading with purpose.

This week is just the beginning. Each day has been designed to spark thought, inspire action, and lead you closer to orchestrating your life's symphony with intent and impact. Stay tuned for Week 2, where we'll explore further chapters and deepen our journey into purposeful resilience.

The Circus Tent

Life often resembles a smoke-and-mirrors spectacle, a dizzying performance where societal expectations and external pressures swirl around us like confetti. But let's dim the blinding spotlight, sweep away the glitter, and expose the illusion. The idea that caring about everything is the secret to a fulfilled existence is a myth—a hollow performance that leaves us exhausted, not enriched.

Authenticity isn't some rare treasure hidden in an unreachable cavern. It's the transformative force that turns the lead of societal conformity into the gold of genuine self-expression. To embrace authenticity means shedding the costumes and masks society hands us. It is about stepping out onto the stage of life not as a performer but as your unvarnished, unapologetic self.

There's a pervasive myth that life comes with a universal checklist—careers, relationships, social status, and even the brand of coffee in your cup. This illusion urges us to care deeply about everything, often at the cost of our own emotional well-being. Authenticity, however, scoffs at this checklist. It invites us to tear it up and write our own, one that prioritizes what truly resonates with our souls.

Imagine that your emotional energy is a currency, one that is finite and precious. Authenticity introduces the concept of a "budget for caring." This isn't about being callous; it's about mindful allocation. Instead of overspending on trivial concerns, authenticity encourages deliberate investment in what truly matters.

Society, like a master puppeteer, loves to pull the strings of our emotions, dictating where we should place our energy and attention. But authenticity hands us a pair of scissors and challenges us to cut those strings. It asks us to reclaim our power and move to the rhythm of our own truth rather than the manipulative tune of societal expectations.

To live authentically is, in many ways, an act of quiet rebellion. It is a refusal to be pressed into the cookie-cutter molds that society creates. Authenticity doesn't seek permission to exist; it bursts through the door with courage and conviction, leaving societal norms quaking in its wake.

But not all concerns carry equal weight. Authenticity teaches us to be discerning, to reserve our energy for the people, causes, and pursuits that align with our values. Everything else? It belongs in the distant periphery, no longer occupying the central stage of our lives.

The world's expectations are like a chaotic circus tent, with crowds clamoring for conformity and performers striving for applause. Authenticity, in this metaphor, is the daring tightrope walker who balances between societal approval and individual truth. It moves gracefully, unshaken by the roar of the crowd, focused instead on the rhythm of its own heart.

Like Dorothy in The Wizard of Oz, we often discover that the "great and powerful" forces we strive to please are mere mortals behind a curtain of illusion. Authenticity pulls back that curtain, exposing the vulnerability and artifice of societal pressures. It reminds us that our worth is not tied to these illusions.

Authenticity is an unmasking—a deliberate shedding of the layers society has draped over us. Picture a masquerade ball where everyone hides behind ornate masks of conformity. Authenticity is the bold soul who removes the mask, inviting others to do the same. This act isn't easy, but it is transformative. It is in unmasking ourselves that we discover the richness of our true identity.

Society often promotes a relentless pursuit of perfection, but this chase is as futile as trying to capture moonlight in your hands. Authenticity rejects the illusion of perfection. Instead, it embraces the beauty in flaws, the strength in vulnerability, and the charm in imperfection. These are the brushstrokes that make your life a masterpiece, vivid and unique.

In the arid desert of societal expectations, authenticity stands as a fountain of renewal. Its waters are refreshing, not because they offer perfection, but because they quench a deeper thirst: the need for genuine self-expression. This fountain reminds us that conformity can never satisfy the longing to be truly seen and heard.

Navigating life without authenticity is like sailing without a compass. It leaves us adrift, unsure of our direction. Authenticity, however, provides the tools we need—a compass to guide us through the landscapes of self-discovery and a map that encourages us to explore the uncharted territories of our true selves.

To embrace authenticity is to gaze into a mirror that reflects not just your appearance but the essence of who you are. This mirror doesn't airbrush imperfections or distort reality. Instead, it celebrates every scar, every wrinkle, every line as a testament to your journey.

Picture a bonfire fueled by societal expectations, its flames dancing in celebration of authenticity. This fire doesn't destroy; it cleanses. It burns away illusions and leaves behind the raw, untamed essence of your true self. Around this fire, there is no judgment, only the warmth of self-acceptance and the light of self-discovery.

Take a moment to make a solemn pledge—a commitment to step out of the circus tent, to dance to your own rhythm, and to care only about what truly aligns with your heart. Authenticity is not a destination but a guiding light, illuminating the path to a life of meaning and purpose.

Key Takeaways
- **Authenticity Is Power:** It's not about rebellion for its own sake but about reclaiming your energy and attention for what truly matters.
- **Discernment Over Perfection:** Not every concern deserves your focus. Save your emotional investment for what aligns with your values.
- **Unmasking the Self:** Removing societal masks is a courageous act that leads to profound self-discovery.
- **Celebrate Imperfection:** True beauty lies in flaws and vulnerability, not in chasing an unattainable ideal.

- **Self-Acceptance:** The only approval that truly matters is your own.

Life is not meant to be lived as a performance under a circus tent. Step outside, let the noise fade, and embrace the wide-open space where authenticity flourishes. The journey begins with a single, bold step toward your truest self. Play your melody, write your story, and let the world marvel at the beauty of your genuine expression.

The Messy Threads That Weave Our Lives

Relationships are the intricate threads that form the tapestry of our lives. Each connection—whether fleeting or enduring—is a vibrant thread contributing to the ever-changing masterpiece of human experience. Like skilled yet imperfect weavers, we are tasked with creating a cohesive design from a chaotic array of connections, shared moments, and occasional tangles. Let's step into life's loom and explore the artistry of relationships.

Relationships are the yarn that forms the very fabric of life. Each thread represents a connection: a laugh shared, a tear shed, or even the quiet understanding of an unspoken moment. Together, these threads create a quilt of warmth and meaning, one that sustains us through life's coldest seasons.

Friendship, for instance, is the lively cha-cha of this weaving dance—a playful rhythm of shared secrets, inside jokes, and mutual support. It's a sanctuary of camaraderie where even missteps are forgiven, and the dance continues with joy. Friendship reminds us that the most meaningful connections often come with a willingness to embrace imperfections.

Acquaintances, on the other hand, are like patches in the tapestry—some vibrant, others subtle, and a few frayed at the edges. Even the smallest patch can add unexpected beauty or lead to a serendipitous adventure. Each has its place, contributing to the rich diversity of life's design.

Trust is the silk thread that binds the tapestry of relationships. Delicate yet resilient, it requires care and attention. A single broken thread can unravel an entire section, yet with patience and effort, it can often be mended. Trust forms the foundation of strong relationships, where openness and vulnerability are celebrated rather than feared.

Shared moments act as the stitches holding the tapestry together. They are the belly laughs over silly jokes, the quiet solidarity during difficult times, and the spontaneous adventures that fill life with color. Bold stitches—like shared dreams or deep conversations—often create the most intricate and beautiful designs.

Weaving relationships requires balance. Life demands we juggle threads of work, family, friends, and personal time—a delicate act akin to juggling flaming torches while riding a unicycle. Yet, when balance is achieved, the satisfaction of harmonizing these threads is unmatched.

Boundaries are the tension ropes of the weaving process. Sometimes, the loom requires a firm tug to set clear limits and protect your emotional space. Other times, a gentler touch allows others to draw closer. The art of boundary-setting lies in knowing when to tighten and when to loosen the threads, creating a balance of give and take that strengthens the overall design.

Family threads run deep, forming the intricate embroidery of our tapestry. These threads are often more elaborate and interwoven, connecting generations and shaping the stories we tell. They may be complex and occasionally frayed, but they add depth and character to the design. The quirks and imperfections of family are not flaws—they're the unique patterns that make the tapestry unmistakably ours.

Laughter is the joyful symphony playing in the background of life's loom. Whether it's the melodic laughter of friends or the hearty guffaws of family, it creates a rhythm that brightens the tapestry. Let laughter echo through your relationships, filling the empty spaces with joy.

Equally important is solitude, a patch in the tapestry often overlooked. Like the negative space in a painting, solitude enhances the beauty of the whole. These quiet moments allow for self-reflection and growth, providing the clarity needed to weave stronger connections with others.

Conflict is the dramatic plot twist in the Tapestry of Relationships. Like tension in a story, it challenges the strength of the threads and often leads to unexpected growth. Avoiding conflict weakens the weave, while addressing it with empathy and communication strengthens the bonds.

Change, too, is an essential element in the weaving process. It's the dye that alters the hues of the tapestry, sometimes subtly and other times with bold, unexpected splashes of color. Embrace these evolving shades—they add richness, depth, and vibrancy to the design.

Support is the warmth that radiates from the tapestry. It's the cozy quilt that wraps around us when life feels cold. Be that source of comfort for others, and allow them to do the same for you. A network of supportive relationships weaves together a fabric that is both resilient and nurturing.

Tangles are inevitable in the weaving process. Threads get knotted, relationships fray, and misunderstandings arise. The untangling process requires patience, communication, and often a dose of humor. These moments of imperfection, when resolved with care, create patterns that tell a story of perseverance and connection.

In today's world, social media adds a mosaic-like quality to our tapestry. Digital threads connect us across distances, creating opportunities for new relationships and shared experiences. Yet, like any thread, they must be used mindfully. Too much digital noise can obscure the warmth of face-to-face connections. Balance is key.

Shared goals act as the quilt squares that align the threads of relationships. When people come together with a common purpose, their collaboration creates a unified and beautiful design. Identify these shared goals in your tapestry, and stitch them with intention and care.

Key Takeaways
- **Trust and Shared Moments:** Trust is the silk that binds, and shared experiences are the stitches that strengthen relationships.

- **Balance and Boundaries:** Relationships thrive on a delicate balance of connection and individuality, supported by healthy boundaries.
- **Family and Friendship:** Each type of relationship contributes its unique texture, from the intricate embroidery of family to the playful rhythm of friendship.
- **Conflict and Change:** Growth often comes from tension and transformation. Embrace both as integral to the tapestry of life.
- **Support and Solitude:** Relationships flourish when nurtured by mutual support and enriched by moments of solitude.

Step back and admire the masterpiece you are weaving—the Tapestry of Relationships. Each thread, knot, and patch tells a story of connection, growth, and resilience. Keep weaving, cherishing the vibrant threads that bring warmth, beauty, and meaning to the fabric of your life.

The Echo Chamber

The echo chamber is a deceptive sanctuary—a comfortable space where your beliefs are mirrored back to you, unchallenged and uninterrupted. It offers the soothing lull of familiarity, but comfort can be a dangerous melody, one that lulls you into stagnation. Growth demands more than repetition; it requires the sharp notes of challenge, the jarring dissonance of opposing ideas.

Validation within the echo chamber is a mirage, a shimmering illusion that tricks you into believing you're advancing. In reality, growth thrives not in comfort but in the fertile soil of discomfort. It is in confronting the unfamiliar and wrestling with dissent that you uncover deeper truths about yourself and the world around you.

Inside the echo chamber, every note sounds familiar, creating a repetitive symphony that soothes but does not inspire. Life, however, is meant to be a dynamic composition, filled with crescendos, unexpected harmonies, and even discordant clashes that ultimately lead to richer understanding.

The echo chamber is a playground for the ego, where it reigns unchallenged as the star of every performance. Here, the ego thrives on validation, basking in the glow of agreement and unexamined praise. Yet, this stage is not the arena of authentic growth. True evolution requires vulnerability—stepping off the ego's pedestal and embracing the humility that comes with being challenged.

Great stories are rarely solitary endeavors. In the echo chamber, you may be the writer, director, and protagonist, but real growth requires a diverse cast of characters. Collaboration, disagreement, and fresh perspectives add richness to the narrative of your life.

Too much comfort is akin to still waters—it feels safe but slowly stagnates. Growth, on the other hand, is found in the unpredictable currents of challenge and diversity. Making waves, disrupting the stillness, and embracing discomfort are essential acts of self-discovery.

Validation and growth are often mistaken as partners, but they can be fierce adversaries. Validation soothes, while growth disrupts. The choice is yours: to remain in the safety of agreement or to venture into the unknown in pursuit of personal evolution.

The echo chamber thrives on a feedback loop of validation, where familiar beliefs are echoed back to you, creating an illusion of progress. To grow, you must disrupt this pattern. Invite dissonance, for it is the precursor to harmony. True understanding emerges not from uniformity but from the tension of opposing ideas.

Stagnation waits in the shadows of the echo chamber, preying on those unwilling to step into the discomfort of change. But beyond the chamber lies the uncharted territory of growth. The path may be uncertain, but it is brimming with potential.

The echo chamber is seductive, a siren's call urging you to stay within the confines of the known. Yet, life's most transformative experiences often lie beyond the familiar. Resisting the comfort of validation and stepping into the wilderness of self-discovery is a bold but necessary act.

In the echo chamber, validation can become a crutch, supporting your beliefs but weakening your ability to stand firmly in self-awareness. True strength comes from letting go of the need for constant agreement and learning to stand tall on your own foundation.

Disagreement is often seen as a threat, but it is, in truth, a powerful catalyst for growth. Within the clash of ideas lies the potential for deeper understanding. The fear of dissent is a specter haunting the echo chamber, but confronting it leads to liberation.

Echoes are weak whispers, bouncing back the same sounds. True achievement resounds like a thunderclap, powerful and far-reaching. To trade echoes for resonance, you must break free from the chamber and embrace the challenge of authentic growth.

The echo chamber is a fragile bubble, an illusion of safety. Yet, bubbles inevitably burst. When they do, the shards of illusion can pave the way for the solid ground of authenticity. Growth is not a monotonous drone but a vibrant symphony, rich with contrasts and crescendos.

Discomfort, far from being an enemy, is the catalyst for growth. It is the fertilizer that nourishes the seeds of progress, turning the awkward and the uneasy into the blossoming of potential.

The harmony of agreement in the echo chamber is a myth—a shallow unity devoid of depth. True unity is found in the cacophony of diverse voices, where each perspective adds a unique note to the symphony of understanding.

Authenticity thrives in the wild, uncharted terrains beyond the chamber, where validation is not a prerequisite. It is here, in the untamed spaces, that you find the courage to prioritize the authenticity of your journey over the comforting applause of agreement.

Disagreement is not a prison but a key—one that unlocks the door to liberation. By stepping into the unknown, you discover the freedom that comes from embracing diverse perspectives and challenging your assumptions.

Mark your departure from the echo chamber. Beyond its walls lies a horizon brimming with possibilities—a symphony of life's most dynamic and authentic notes. Break the sound barrier of self-validation and listen for the crescendo of growth, connection, and understanding.

Key Takeaways
- **Challenge Comfort:** Growth lies beyond the soothing rhythm of agreement. Discomfort is a necessary catalyst for progress.
- **Disrupt the Loop:** Escape the feedback loop of validation by inviting diverse perspectives and embracing dissent.

- **Dim the Ego's Spotlight:** True evolution requires humility and vulnerability, not the constant reassurance of unchallenged beliefs.
- **Seek Resonance, Not Echoes:** Let go of weak validations and strive for the thunderclap of authentic achievement.
- Step Into the Unknown: The path beyond the echo chamber is uncharted but filled with potential for genuine transformation.

The echoes are fading, and the music of your growth awaits. Step boldly into the symphony of authenticity, where each note, clash, and crescendo contributes to the masterpiece of your life. The horizon ahead is vast and filled with the promise of true evolution. Listen closely—the crescendo is calling.

Not Your Grandma's Etiquette Class

Welcome to a bold exploration of boundaries and the transformative power of "no." This isn't a quaint lesson in manners but a revolutionary guide to reclaiming your autonomy, preserving your peace, and curating a life aligned with your priorities. Saying no isn't an act of rejection—it's an assertion of self-worth and intentional living. It's time to master the art of no with finesse, confidence, and just a hint of rebellion.

In a culture that glorifies relentless yeses, a single well-placed no is an act of defiance. Saying no doesn't make you a naysayer; it makes you a curator of your time, energy, and attention. Each refusal is a brushstroke on the canvas of your life, crafting a masterpiece that reflects your values and aspirations.

Saying no isn't about negativity; it's about clarity. Imagine your life as a grand orchestra, where each no is the conductor's baton directing focus to the essential notes. In the symphony of intentional living, no orchestrates harmony by silencing the noise of overcommitment.

Saying no is a skill, a graceful dance that combines assertiveness with consideration. It's the no-guilt two-step: the rhythm of self-care unburdened by unnecessary apologies. Every refusal is a confident step toward honoring your boundaries and embracing your needs.

Let your no be a shield of self-care. Saying no isn't rejection—it's safeguarding your energy, your mental health, and your time. This is the essence of unapologetic self-preservation, where your boundaries serve as the fortress protecting your well-being.

Learning to say no is like mastering a new language—a dialect of honesty and respect. It's not about being rude; it's about communicating with clarity. Expand your no vocabulary with phrases like:

- "I appreciate the opportunity, but I can't commit right now."
- "This doesn't align with my current priorities."
- "I have to decline to ensure I can honor my existing commitments."

These responses convey respect while firmly establishing your boundaries.

Injecting humor into your no repertoire can also disarm tension. A touch of wit turns a refusal into a moment of levity. For example, "I'd love to help, but I'm on a strict no-overcommitment diet—doctor's orders!" Humor softens the blow while reinforcing your decision.

Picture yourself as an artist sculpting boundaries with precision. Your toolkit includes:

- **The Chisel of Assertiveness:** Carve out clear limits with confidence.
- **The Brush of Clarity:** Paint your intentions with honesty and kindness.
- **The Hammer of Conviction:** Reinforce your boundaries with unwavering self-respect.

Boundaries are not barriers but frameworks that allow you to show up fully and authentically in every aspect of your life.

Not every request deserves a no, but those that encroach on your well-being demand swift and purposeful refusal. Like a Zen master in the dojo of life, practice the art of selective no's. Choose your battles wisely, and when necessary, let your no be as decisive as a sword cutting through the unnecessary.

In relationships, a well-crafted no can strengthen connections rather than weaken them. Frame your refusals with care, like a love letter to yourself and others: "I value our connection deeply, but I need to honor my own needs as well." Such communication balances honesty with consideration, maintaining respect while asserting boundaries.

Think of no as your weapon in the guerrilla warfare of time management. Each refusal is a strategic move, reclaiming precious hours for what truly matters. Wield your no with purpose, striking down time-wasting obligations and opening space for meaningful pursuits.

Saying no is not a shackle; it's a key to liberation. It frees you from the chains of people-pleasing and the weight of overcommitment. With every no, you unlock the door to a life where your priorities and well-being take center stage.

A single no is never solitary. Like a stone cast into water, it sends ripples through your life, encouraging others to honor their own boundaries. Your act of self-respect creates a ripple effect, inspiring a collective culture of intentionality and authenticity.

The art of saying no is a marathon, not a sprint. It requires practice, patience, and perseverance. Like a runner building endurance, you strengthen your boundary muscles with every refusal. Over time, no becomes less daunting and more empowering.

Each no contributes to your personal anthem—a resounding declaration of self-worth and intentionality. Imagine it as a melody that echoes through your decisions, reinforcing your commitment to a life of clarity and purpose.

Every no contains a hidden yes—a yes to your priorities, your peace, and your authentic self. Saying no is not about closing doors; it's about opening the right ones. With each refusal, you align your choices with your values, paving the way for a life that resonates with your true desires.

Boundaries are not static; they shift and grow with the seasons of your life. The art of saying no is an ever-evolving masterpiece, a dynamic creation that adapts to new challenges and opportunities. Embrace the fluidity of your boundaries, letting each no be a stroke on the ever-changing canvas of your unapologetic existence.

Key Takeaways

- **No as Empowerment:** Saying no is not rejection but an assertion of self-worth and clarity.
- **Refusal with Grace:** Develop a language of no that balances honesty with respect and humor.
- **Selective Nos:** Practice the art of purposeful refusals, focusing on what protects your peace and aligns with your values.
- **Time Liberation:** Use no as a strategic tool to reclaim your time and energy.
- **Ever-Evolving Boundaries:** Let your boundaries adapt as you grow, creating a masterpiece of intentional living.

Master the rebellious art of saying no. With each refusal, you sculpt a life of purpose, clarity, and authenticity. Let your no's resonate as declarations of self-respect, and watch as they open doors to a richer, more intentional existence. The symphony of your life deserves nothing less than the masterpiece of well-chosen priorities. Play on.

The Cookie-Cutter Catastrophe

Life is not a clearance sale, and you are far from a mass-produced item. It's time to unravel the stifling garment of the "One Size Fits All" mentality and embrace the bespoke beauty of your individuality. This chapter is a rallying cry against conformity—a celebration of quirks, eccentricities, and the glorious chaos that makes each of us irreplaceably unique.

The "One Size Fits All" mentality is a cookie-cutter catastrophe, an illusion that insists humanity must conform to identical molds. It suggests that we think, feel, and live in the same way, as if life were a factory line churning out carbon copies. But life is not a conveyor belt, and you are not a widget. You are an intricate, one-of-a-kind creation, and it's time to embrace that truth.

Happiness, like individuality, cannot be mass-produced. There is no universal formula for joy, no standardized blueprint for fulfillment. What brings one person happiness might leave another unfulfilled. Your happiness is a bespoke creation, stitched together from the threads of your passions, dreams, and desires. It's time to let go of the idea that your joy must fit into someone else's mold.

Life isn't a scripted play where everyone recites the same lines. It's an improv performance, and you are both the writer and the star of your show. The "One Size Fits All" mindset hands you a generic script, but true fulfillment comes from crafting your narrative. Grab the pen and write a story that resonates with your unique voice.

Imagine life as a bespoke suit tailored to your exact measurements. Each seam, stitch, and detail reflects your essence. Trying to fit into someone else's ill-fitting attire not only diminishes your authenticity but also stifles your potential. Tailor your life to the contours of your soul, and wear it unapologetically.

Averageness is the enemy of exceptional. The "One Size Fits All" mentality celebrates mediocrity, leaving no room for outliers, innovators, or dreamers. Yet, it is our quirks and peculiarities that make us extraordinary. Let's celebrate the absurdity that is each of us—gloriously unique and magnificently peculiar.

Eccentricity is the spice of life, the vibrant color in an otherwise monotonous existence. Your quirks and oddities are not flaws; they are your signature. Let the world marvel at the kaleidoscope of your individuality.

The "One Size Fits All" mentality functions like a straitjacket, binding you to societal expectations of behavior, success, and timelines. It dictates when you should achieve milestones, what success should look like, and how you should live. But life's timeline is subjective, and success is deeply personal. Walk to the beat of your own drum, and let society's expectations fall by the wayside.

Labels are another tool of conformity—uniform badges in the "One Size Fits All" army. Peel them off. You are not a product on a shelf but a nuanced masterpiece, painted with the hues of your experiences and beliefs. Refuse to be confined by the limitations of labels.

Unapologetic uniqueness is an art form. There's no need to apologize for being who you are. Your individuality is your strength, your masterpiece. Embrace your quirks, flaunt your eccentricities, and revel in the vivid spectrum of your existence.

Conformity, by contrast, is the conveyor belt of a mundane life. It keeps you moving in predictable patterns, limiting your potential for growth and exploration. Step off the conveyor belt and forge your own path, one that reflects your passions and priorities.

Relationships, like individuals, aren't cut from the same cloth. The "One Size Fits All" mentality assumes that connections must conform to societal norms, but the truth is far richer. Your relationships are a patchwork quilt, each square representing a unique bond woven together by shared experiences and mutual understanding.

Emotions, too, defy uniformity. They are not monochrome; they are a vibrant spectrum of hues that color the canvas of your life. Let yourself feel the full range of emotions, from the deepest blues of sorrow to the brightest yellows of joy. Life is richer in technicolor than in grayscale.

The comparison trap is a cornerstone of the "One Size Fits All" mentality, luring you into measuring your life against others. But your journey is your own—a bespoke trail winding through landscapes unique to your experiences and choices. Walk it with pride and purpose, refusing to let comparison diminish your individuality.

Your beliefs, like your life, should be tailor-made. Reject the idea that you must adopt a pre-packaged set of beliefs to fit in. Choose the convictions that resonate with your soul, even if they clash with societal norms.

Life is a blank canvas, and the "One Size Fits All" mentality hands you a paint-by-numbers kit. But conformity stifles creativity. Splash bold strokes of your dreams, passions, and eccentricities onto your canvas. Create a masterpiece that defies boundaries, a vibrant celebration of your unique spirit.

Wisdom, too, is not universal. It's a fluid, adaptable force that takes shape according to your individual journey. Seek out wisdom that aligns with your path, not the one-size-fits-all platitudes offered by society.

Key Takeaways
- **Reject Conformity:** Life is not a conveyor belt. Embrace your individuality and walk your own path.
- **Celebrate Eccentricity:** Your quirks and oddities are not flaws; they are the essence of your uniqueness.
- **Tailor Your Happiness:** Joy is not one-size-fits-all. Craft a life that aligns with your passions and desires.
- **Break Free from Labels:** Refuse to be confined by societal expectations and labels. Create your own identity.

- **Revel in Unapologetic Uniqueness:** Celebrate your individuality and let it shine as your greatest strength.

The "One Size Fits All" mentality is a disservice to the vibrant mosaic of humanity. Life wasn't meant to be uniform; it is a kaleidoscope of individual narratives. So, cast off the constraints of conformity, embrace your eccentricities, and let the world marvel at the masterpiece that is your unapologetic existence.

Week 2

Week 2 Action Plan: Cultivating Connections and Creative Chaos

Welcome to Week 2 of "Orchestrating Impact: Conducting Life's Symphony with Purpose and Resilience." This week, we delve into the heart of human connections, embrace the beauty of creative chaos, and learn to navigate the complex emotional landscapes of our lives. Let's continue to build your resilience and impact with purpose.

Day 1: "The Art of Creative Chaos"
- **Activity:** Identify a current problem or project. Spend 30 minutes brainstorming creative, unconventional solutions or ideas. Embrace wild, out-of-the-box thinking without judgment.
- **Reflection:** How did embracing creative chaos shift your perspective or approach?

Day 2: "The Jungle of Human Connection"
- **Activity:** Reach out to someone with whom you want to deepen your connection. This could be through a meaningful conversation, a shared activity, or a heartfelt message.
- **Reflection:** Reflect on the nature of this connection. How does it contribute to your life's symphony?

Day 3: "The Unhealthy Connections"
- **Activity:** Reflect on your relationships and identify any that may be draining or counterproductive to your well-being. Plan a gentle but firm conversation or action to redefine or release these connections.
- **Reflection:** How does the process of addressing or releasing unhealthy connections make you feel?

Day 4: "The Emotional Stock Exchange"
- **Activity:** Track your emotional investments throughout the day. Note moments or interactions that significantly lift or lower your spirits. Evaluate if these investments align with your values and goals.
- **Reflection:** Which emotional investments are yielding positive returns, and which are costing you?

Day 5: "Forging Your Own Path"
- **Activity:** Spend time visualizing your ideal path forward in life or career. Create a vision board or write a detailed description of this path, focusing on what feels authentic and fulfilling.
- **Reflection:** In what ways does this vision challenge the status quo of your current trajectory?

Day 6: "The Drumbeat You Can't Ignore"
- **Activity:** Identify a passion or cause that resonates deeply with you but you've been neglecting. Outline the first three steps you can take to integrate this more fully into your life.
- **Reflection:** How does focusing on this passion or cause reinvigorate your sense of purpose?

Day 7: Weekly Integration
- **Activity:** Review your activities and reflections from the week. Write a letter to your future self, describing what you've learned and how you hope to apply these insights moving forward.

- **Reflection:** Reflect on the growth you've experienced this week. How has your understanding of human connections and creative chaos deepened?

This week has been a journey through the landscapes of connection and creativity, crucial components of orchestrating impact with resilience. Each step taken is a note added to your symphony, enriching its melody and harmony. Prepare for Week 3, where we will explore further dimensions of your purpose and resilience.

The Art of Creative Chaos

In a world dominated by reactive problem-solving, we've become accustomed to playing defense, dodging life's curveballs, and extinguishing fires. But this approach keeps us stuck in a loop, solving the same problems with the same methods, never daring to imagine something different. It's time for a revolution—a revolution that champions the brilliance of proactive, creative chaos.

This isn't about crisis management. It's about stepping into the unknown, igniting your own flames of innovation, and dancing fearlessly in their glow.

Reactive problem-solving is the hamster wheel of life, a monotonous cycle of catch-up that keeps us tethered to the past. It's like living on a merry-go-round of monotony—round and round you go, addressing the same issues, patching the same leaks. But temporary fixes are no substitute for transformation.

It's time to step off the wheel, take a sledgehammer to the merry-go-round, and choose a new path. Proactive problem-solving doesn't wait for the problem to arrive; it anticipates, imagines, and prepares for the unexpected. It's not just about solutions; it's about creating a foundation where the problems themselves can be reimagined.

Think of proactive problem-solving as an act of rebellion against convention. It's a declaration of independence from predictable thinking and a manifesto for bold, audacious innovation. Proactive thinkers don't just navigate the maze—they rise above it, seeing the entire picture and plotting their own course.

The essence of proactive problem-solving is creativity—embracing the chaotic, unexpected, and even absurd ideas that come from the wild edges of your imagination. This is the art of creative chaos, where logic meets lunacy to produce solutions that are as daring as they are effective.

Creative chaos is where the magic happens. It's the sandbox where you allow yourself to dream the impossible, question the unquestionable, and imagine the unimaginable.

- **Curiosity:** Start by asking "What if?" Let your mind wander to places others might consider ridiculous. The best solutions often hide in the realm of the unexpected.
- **Courage:** Dare to challenge norms and take risks. Fear is the enemy of innovation; bravery fuels creativity.
- **Imagination:** Blend logic with whimsy, and don't be afraid to let your ideas get a little messy. Messy often leads to magnificent.

Proactive problem-solving isn't about tidiness. It's about rolling up your sleeves, getting your hands dirty, and creating a masterpiece on a paint-splattered canvas of uncertainty.

Every problem is an invitation to innovate. When you embrace proactive problem-solving, you stop seeing obstacles as dead ends. Instead, they become detours on the road to creativity. Problems are not there to halt your progress; they're there to stretch your mind and expand your perspective.

Consider problems as the dissonant notes in life's symphony. Your job is to take these clashing sounds and orchestrate them into a harmonious masterpiece. Each problem, no matter how chaotic, contains the seeds of a solution waiting to be discovered.

To thrive in creative chaos, you need the right tools:

- **Perspective:** Step back and view problems from multiple angles. Like a bird soaring above a maze, gain a new vantage point to see possibilities others miss.
- **Adaptability:** Be ready to pivot. In chaos, plans rarely unfold perfectly. Flexibility is your greatest asset.
- **Collaboration:** Invite diverse perspectives into the mix. Solutions often emerge when differing ideas collide.

Life's challenges are puzzles, and you're the irreverent jester piecing them together with creativity and humor. Forget trying to fit into someone else's picture; craft your own collage, complete with unexpected brilliance and personal flair.

Proactive problem-solving rewrites the rulebook—or tosses it out entirely. Rules often limit innovation. By breaking them, you discover new paths through life's labyrinth.

Think of life as a chaotic circus, with problems as unruly acts demanding attention. Proactive problem-solving doesn't tame the chaos; it transforms it into an exhilarating performance where you call the shots.

Sherlock Holmes didn't solve mysteries by following linear steps; he thrived on the unexpected. Proactive problem-solving invites you to embrace a similar mindset:

- Look beyond the obvious.
- Connect seemingly unrelated dots.
- Use wit and curiosity to unravel challenges.

Each solution becomes a creative triumph, a testament to your ability to think differently.

Proactive problem-solving is a daredevil's dance with the unknown. It turns fear into fuel and challenges into opportunities for audacious feats. It's not about tiptoeing around dilemmas but about diving into them headfirst with a mischievous grin and a fearless heart.

In the hands of a proactive problem-solver, the toolbox isn't just filled with the usual suspects—hammers and nails are joined by glitter, duct tape, and perhaps even a rubber chicken. The essence of proactive problem-solving lies in embracing the unconventional and wielding it with style. Let's dive into the colorful chaos, crafting solutions that don't just solve problems but dazzle in their audacity.

When life sets your carefully laid plans ablaze, reactive problem-solving may have you scrambling for a fire extinguisher. Proactive problem-solving, however, invites you to rise from the ashes like a phoenix, turning disaster into opportunity. It's not about extinguishing the fire; it's about learning the flamenco in its glow. Burn, rise, dance—repeat.

Proactive thinkers understand that the dance of adversity is where transformation happens. Problems don't just challenge—they refine, pushing you to reimagine your approach and create something extraordinary from the unexpected.

Picture your challenges as an audience, skeptically watching your every move. Proactive problem-solving is your moment to take the stage and perform a magic show they'll never forget. It's not about pulling rabbits from hats but about creating moments of surprise and delight that make problems disappear in a puff of creative brilliance.

This is the art of misdirection: reframing problems so they no longer hold power over you. By shifting your focus, you find possibilities where none seemed to exist before.

Life often feels like a circus, complete with juggling acts and unpredictable stunts. Proactive problem-solving transforms you into a comedic genius, tossing challenges in the air with a wink and a smile. Drops are inevitable, but in the world of creative chaos, they're not failures—they're opportunities to improvise and land unexpected punchlines.

By embracing the absurdity of life's messiness, you turn errors into enhancements and setbacks into stepping stones. The circus isn't something to survive—it's your stage to thrive.

If quantum physics teaches us anything, it's that uncertainty is fertile ground for discovery. Proactive problem-solving thrives in this unpredictability, turning the unknown into a canvas for groundbreaking solutions.

Think of it as your quantum quotient: the ability to embrace the chaos and let it lead you to possibilities you couldn't have imagined. By defying the gravity of conventional thinking, you transform uncertainty into innovation.

Life hands you a mixtape of challenges—some dissonant, others harmonious. Proactive problem-solving is your opportunity to remix the chaos, adding your own rhythm and beats. It's not about following the same tired tracks; it's about creating a playlist that inspires you to move boldly through life's unpredictability.

When you dance to the beat of your own solutions, you inspire others to do the same. Creativity becomes contagious, spreading energy and momentum wherever it's applied.

Proactive problem-solving is the Zen of Zest—a philosophy that turns challenges into the spice of life. It's not about settling for bland, safe solutions but about adding just the right amount of irreverent flavor to make your approach extraordinary.

This isn't about recklessness; it's about intentional boldness. It's about finding joy in the unexpected, savoring the twists and turns, and transforming ordinary obstacles into opportunities for growth and wonder.

Life's challenges can feel like turbulent skies, but proactive problem-solving teaches you to soar above the storm. Like an aviator navigating rough weather, you rise into the chaos, not to avoid it but to embrace it with skill and grace.

Proactive problem-solvers don't fear the clouds—they find beauty in them. Each challenge becomes an opportunity to ascend higher, learning to dance among the turbulence and discover clearer skies beyond.

Alchemy turns base metals into gold, and proactive problem-solving transforms adversity into resilience. It's not about avoiding the hard times; it's about transmuting them into the building blocks of strength and innovation.

By sipping from the alchemist's cup, you find the elixir that turns obstacles into opportunities. Every challenge is a chance to refine your approach, hone your creativity, and emerge stronger than before.

Life's journey is rarely smooth. The trails are often unpaved, filled with unexpected nuts and berries. Proactive problem-solving is your trail mix—a blend of unexpected resources and creative ideas that sustain you along the way.

This approach isn't about walking the beaten path; it's about forging your own. Every challenge becomes a snack for your ingenuity, fueling your journey to new horizons.

Proactive problem-solving invites you to craft a vision board of solutions. Unlike traditional vision boards, this one isn't constrained by what's already been done. It's a mosaic of dreams and aspirations woven together with creativity and ambition.

Let your imagination guide you, pasting bold ideas onto your vision board, no matter how unconventional. The unexpected often holds the keys to transformative solutions.

Inventors thrive in the world of spontaneity, where proactive problem-solving takes center stage as an improv session. It's not about rigid scripts; it's about embracing the unexpected and turning hiccups into brilliance.

Welcome to the theater of audacious solutions, where your ingenuity takes the spotlight. Every twist in the plot is an opportunity to surprise, delight, and innovate.

Key Takeaways

- **Break the Cycle:** Reactive problem-solving keeps you in a loop. Proactive thinking liberates you to explore new possibilities.
- **Embrace Creative Chaos:** Innovation thrives in the messy, unpredictable spaces where logic and imagination collide.
- **Transform Problems:** See challenges not as barriers but as opportunities to innovate and grow.
- **Rewrite the Rules:** Question conventions and explore paths others are too afraid to take.
- **Find Joy in the Chaos:** Proactive problem-solving isn't just about solutions; it's about the thrill of discovery and creation.
- **Craft Your Vision:** Build a vision board of bold, unconventional solutions that inspire transformative action.
- **Perform with Flair:** Approach life's circus with humor, ingenuity, and a willingness to improvise.

This is your invitation to become a maestro of creative chaos. Step boldly into the unpredictable, and let your imagination light the way. As you move forward, you'll find solutions that inspire, surprise, and delight—not just you, but the world around you. Get ready to orchestrate your magnum opus in the symphony of life's chaos.

The Jungle of Human Connection

In a world where social media often serves as a shallow substitute for genuine interaction, it's easy to mistake likes, emojis, and heart reactions for meaningful connection. But human relationships, like the deep waters of the ocean, hold treasures that go far beyond the surface. It's time to unplug, dive in, and explore the richness of real connections—those forged through vulnerability, laughter, and shared experiences.

Small talk is the fast food of human interaction: quick, convenient, and ultimately unsatisfying. While it has its place, real connection lies in the hearty feast of deeper conversations. Stories, shared truths, and unfiltered honesty add flavor to relationships, making them nourishing and memorable.

Let's toss the superficial salad aside and serve up a buffet of genuine connection. Ask meaningful questions. Share your triumphs and failures. These are the moments that create lasting bonds, the moments where two souls truly meet.

Picture vulnerability as a superhero cape—not a symbol of weakness, but of immense strength. It takes courage to remove your armor and reveal your authentic self. Yet, this is the foundation of real connection. Vulnerability invites others to do the same, creating a bridge of trust and mutual understanding.

So, let your vulnerability cape flutter proudly. In relationships, it's the wind that carries you to the uncharted heights of genuine connection.

Friendships and relationships aren't linear paths; they're wild rides, full of twists, turns, and unexpected loops. Like a Ferris wheel, they lift us to new heights and occasionally flip us upside-down. Embrace the unpredictability—this is where the beauty lies.

Shared experiences are the stories we tell around the campfire of connection. Triumphs, failures, and bizarre plot twists become the threads that weave the fabric of our relationships. The more we share, the richer the tapestry becomes.

Relationships aren't about fitting square pegs into round holes. They're about celebrating differences—the quirks, idiosyncrasies, and unique perspectives that make each person a distinct puzzle piece. These differences aren't obstacles; they're opportunities to learn, grow, and create something greater together.

The goal isn't to solve the puzzle but to let it unfold naturally. Compatibility develops through shared experiences, trial and error, and mutual understanding.

Relationships thrive on balance, a harmonious dance of give and take. Whether it's the supportive waltz, the playful jitterbug, or the steadfast tango, reciprocity forms the rhythm of genuine connection.

This dance isn't about keeping score; it's about moving in harmony. Listen, support, and allow others to do the same for you. Together, you create a choreography that's as dynamic as it is meaningful.

Curiosity is the compass that guides us through the jungle of human connection. By showing authentic interest in another person's passions, stories, and dreams, you unlock the door to deeper understanding.

Empathy is the rollercoaster ride of human emotion. It plunges you into the depths of someone else's sorrows and lifts you to the peaks of their joys. It's exhilarating, challenging, and profoundly rewarding. The more you lean into the loops and twists, the stronger your connections become.

Trust is the lighthouse that guides relationships through stormy seas. Built on the rock of reliability, it shines through uncertainties, illuminating the way forward. Cultivate trust through consistency, honesty, and support—it's the foundation on which lasting connections are built.

Laughter, on the other hand, is the chorus that reverberates through the aquarium of connection. It swims through the coral reefs of inside jokes and dives into the deep waters of shared humor. Laughter doesn't just echo; it bonds, brightens, and strengthens.

Communication is the finely tuned telescope that brings distant thoughts into focus. Active listening polishes the lens, while clear articulation adjusts the focus. Through this telescope, you explore the vast cosmos of another person's mind, bridging gaps and building shared understanding.

Avoid the broken lens of assumptions or the blurry vision of miscommunication. Instead, invest in clarity, patience, and the art of truly hearing another person's perspective.

Connections are not potted plants, confined and limited. They're sprawling gardens, full of opportunities for mutual growth. By planting seeds of encouragement, watering them with shared aspirations, and cultivating them with understanding, you create a vibrant landscape of support and collaboration.

As each relationship grows, the entire garden flourishes, becoming a living testament to the power of connection.

Dreams aren't meant to be solitary campfires—they're collective bonfires. When people come together to share their ambitions, each spark contributes to a blaze that lights the way for everyone. Around the bonfire of connection, dreams take flight, illuminating shared paths toward common goals.

Life is a symphony of connections, constantly evolving with comings and goings. Each farewell becomes the prelude to a new hello, and every interaction contributes to the melody. Embrace the ebb and flow, cherish the moments of harmony, and let the symphony play on.

Key Takeaways

- **Vulnerability is Strength:** Showing your true self is the cornerstone of genuine connection.

- **Celebrate Differences:** Relationships are enriched by diversity, not uniformity.
- **Reciprocity is Key:** Balance the dance of give and take to create harmony in your connections.
- **Curiosity and Empathy:** These are the guiding stars of meaningful relationships.
- **Build Trust and Share Laughter:** Trust is the foundation, and laughter is the glue of lasting bonds.

Human connection is a jungle—wild, vibrant, and teeming with opportunities for growth and discovery. By navigating it with curiosity, vulnerability, and empathy, you cultivate relationships that enrich your life and the lives of those around you. Step into the jungle with open arms and an open heart, ready to forge connections as extraordinary as the people you meet.

The Unhealthy Connections

Unhealthy connections tether you to emotional patterns that stifle growth and drain vitality. These ties, forged from guilt, misplaced loyalty, or the craving for external validation, cling stubbornly long after their usefulness has passed. Severing these bindings allows you to reclaim your narrative and chart a path toward emotional freedom.

Letting go is not just an act of release—it's an opportunity to transform your emotional world into a space that nurtures resilience, growth, and independence.

Expectations, obligations, and misplaced loyalties often create a web of control, leaving you feeling like a puppet in someone else's show. Grab the scissors of audacity and cut those strings. Life's narrative is yours to script, direct, and perform.

Breaking free from these invisible ties not only liberates you but sets an example for others. Autonomy is not just possible; it is necessary for a life of authenticity and purpose.

Dragging emotional baggage through life feels like hauling an albatross around your neck. Guilt, unresolved pain, and unnecessary attachments weigh heavily, preventing you from soaring. Visualizing the release of these burdens allows your spirit to rise, opening the door to exploration and self-discovery.

The act of untying these knots creates a newfound sense of freedom. Every step forward becomes lighter, each breath more expansive.

Unresolved guilt forges chains that bind you to the past. Learning from guilt, rather than being imprisoned by it, helps to break those chains. Allow guilt to teach its lessons, then release it with gratitude for the insight it provided.

Growth emerges from understanding, not from endless punishment. Reframing guilt as a guide rather than a jailer fosters a healthier relationship with your emotions.

Some individuals thrive by siphoning your energy, leaving you depleted while they flourish. Emotional vampires operate under the guise of charm or neediness, but their impact is unmistakable. Boundaries serve as armor against their draining influence.

Illuminating those boundaries with assertiveness drives away emotional vampires, allowing you to preserve your energy for connections that uplift and support your well-being.

Unmet expectations trap you in cycles of frustration and disappointment. Lighting the torch of self-determination burns down those traps, freeing you to walk a path of your own choosing.

Embracing life's unpredictability allows for growth and joy in unexpected places. Letting go of rigid expectations creates space for genuine fulfillment.

Attachments can feel thrilling, like a bungee jump where the tether prevents the fall. However, cutting the cord delivers a deeper sense of exhilaration—the freedom of soaring untethered. Letting go offers the chance to discover new heights, free from the entanglements of dependency.

True freedom arises when you release the need to hold onto what no longer serves you. The updrafts of independence carry you higher than fear ever allowed.

Drama often masquerades as excitement, drawing you in with promises of thrill but delivering only turmoil. Redirecting your energy toward peace and contentment steers you away from stormy seas.

The calm waters of stability reveal a richer, more enduring joy. Choosing tranquility over chaos fosters a life of clarity and balance.

Resentment consumes energy, feeding on old grievances and keeping you locked in the past. Allowing the fire of resentment to burn out fertilizes the soil for forgiveness and renewal.

New growth emerges in the absence of resentment's flames. Forgiveness isn't about forgetting but about reclaiming energy for the future and nurturing the seeds of possibility.

An emotional house of cards, though intricate, teeters precariously and demands constant maintenance. Letting it collapse provides an opportunity to rebuild with resilience and wisdom. Using bricks of authenticity and mutual respect strengthens connections, allowing them to withstand life's inevitable challenges. Strong foundations support meaningful relationships that thrive under pressure.

The need for external validation creates a self-imposed prison, keeping you captive to others' opinions. Seeking approval from within breaks this cycle, allowing you to find confidence in your own worth.

Self-reliance brings freedom from the constant chase for acknowledgment. Walking into the sunlight of self-acceptance shines light on the power you hold to define your value.

Life often feels like a relentless tug-of-war with emotions that drain your energy without purpose. Dropping the rope isn't surrender; it's a conscious choice to step out of unnecessary battles and reclaim your peace. Conflict is not mandatory. Choosing to disengage from emotional skirmishes is an act of empowerment.

Grudges act as stones in an emotional backpack, weighing you down and slowing your progress. Unloading this weight clears the path ahead, allowing you to continue your journey with lightness and freedom. Instead of hoarding resentment, collect memories of joy, lessons learned, and moments of forgiveness. These treasures are far more sustaining than the burden of past grievances.

Letting go doesn't erase the past, but it transforms how you carry it. By releasing the heavy stones of anger and regret, you create space for the beauty of the present.

Comparison often lures you into the trap of self-doubt, convincing you to measure your worth against others. Planting your feet firmly on the ground of self-appreciation stops this descent into inadequacy. Recognizing the uniqueness of your journey allows you to see your inherent value, rendering comparison irrelevant.

Your path is yours alone, incomparable and worthy. Close the trapdoor of comparison and let it remain sealed, standing tall in the knowledge that your progress is valid and enough.

Emotional chaos can sweep through your life like a tornado, threatening to uproot your stability. Seeking the calm at the eye of the storm offers clarity and strength. Within this space of stillness, balance becomes attainable.

The storm's power diminishes when you focus on your inner calm rather than its destructive force. Emotions may swirl around you, but by anchoring yourself, you find resilience and peace amid the turbulence.

Regret often feels like a rollercoaster, looping endlessly through missed opportunities and what-ifs. Stepping off this ride shifts your focus from the past to the present. Redemption lies in learning from your regrets and using those lessons to guide your choices.

The twists and turns of regret can become a path to growth, allowing you to reclaim agency over your decisions and walk forward with intention.

Unhealthy attachments deserve a farewell. Bury them, grieve their loss, and move on. Life's too precious to dwell in the graveyard of emotional entanglements. A eulogy for these attachments honors the lessons they provided while celebrating your emancipation from their hold.

The freedom gained from releasing these bonds allows your spirit to soar, unshackled and ready to embrace the vast expanse of emotional liberation.

The collapse of fragile emotional structures, though disorienting, clears the way for something stronger. Fragility offers no lasting stability, but its fall provides the opportunity to gather the materials needed for reconstruction.

Sweeping away remnants of these collapses involves more than physical removal. Examining the illusions that once defined you enables you to choose authenticity over ephemerality. Clearing these remnants creates space for enduring values, relationships, and beliefs.

Replacing a house of cards with a fortress built of bricks creates a structure capable of withstanding life's gales. Each brick represents resilience, lessons learned, and wisdom gained. Unlike fragile cards, these bricks hold firm against external pressures.

The foundation of this fortress lies in self-awareness, its walls in self-esteem, and its battlements in unwavering belief in your worth. Within these walls, strength is cultivated not as isolation but as a sanctuary from which you can engage with life more fully.

The design of an emotional fortress reflects individuality. Some may build towering spires of ambition, while others create open courtyards of vulnerability. Each fortress is a testament to personal values and priorities.

Inside, rooms of reflection allow for introspection, halls of celebration commemorate triumphs, and gardens of tranquility nurture peace. These spaces honor every aspect of your emotional self, reminding you that true strength comes from courageously facing life's challenges.

A well-built emotional fortress weathers life's inevitable storms. While the winds may howl and the rain may fall, its foundations remain firm. Challenges are felt but do not break you. Within your fortress, strength, clarity, and peace prevail.

Constructing this sanctuary is a lifelong endeavor. Each experience adds another brick, fortifies a wall, or expands a room. As you grow, so does your fortress, evolving into a reflection of your resilience and wisdom.

An emotional fortress is not meant to shut the world out. Its gates remain open to those who respect its boundaries and honor its creator. Within its walls, deep and meaningful relationships flourish, built on mutual respect and understanding.

Key Takeaways
- **Sever Unhealthy Ties:** Take control of your narrative by cutting the strings of obligations, expectations, and misplaced loyalties.
- Disengage from Unnecessary Battles: Choose peace by stepping away from conflicts that serve no purpose.
- Release Emotional Weight: Let go of grudges and unhealthy attachments to lighten your load and move forward freely.
- **Build Resilience:** Replace fragile structures with a fortress of strength, crafted from self-awareness and hard-earned wisdom.
- **Celebrate Individuality:** Design an emotional sanctuary that reflects your unique values and priorities.
- **Guard Your Energy:** Boundaries protect against emotional vampires and create space for healthier connections.

- **Foster Meaningful Connections:** Invite relationships into your life that align with your boundaries and respect your journey.
- **Validate Yourself:** Internal validation fosters freedom, confidence, and self-reliance.

Unhealthy connections can feel like anchors, keeping you tethered to places you've outgrown. By letting go of these weights, you create room for relationships that align with your growth and values. Begin this journey with intention, and watch your life unfold in new, empowering directions.

Emotional liberation begins with letting go of what no longer serves you. As you clear away the debris of unhealthy connections, you create space for a life built on strength, authenticity, and peace. Step into the sanctuary of your emotional fortress and engage with the world from a place of resilience and clarity.

The Emotional Stock Exchange

Welcome to the emotional stock exchange, where your feelings are the currency, and you are the trader. Here, every decision—every emotional investment, withdrawal, or trade—shapes your inner portfolio. Mastering emotional regulation is akin to navigating the volatile world of Wall Street: it requires strategy, foresight, and a healthy dose of adaptability. With the right tools, you can manage the highs and lows, ensuring your emotional wealth grows steadily over time.

Think of your emotions as stocks, each with its own value and volatility. Happiness might be a blue-chip stock—stable and desirable—while anxiety could be a high-risk, high-reward investment. Emotional regulation is your personal Wall Street, where you decide which emotions to buy into, which to sell, and which to hold for the long haul.

Every day, you play two roles:

- **The Emotional Broker:** Making decisions about where to invest your emotional energy.
- **The Market Analyst:** Observing trends in your feelings and forecasting emotional shifts.

By honing these skills, you can create a balanced portfolio that maximizes your emotional resilience while minimizing unnecessary turmoil.

Emotions, like markets, have their bulls and bears. The bull market of joy is exhilarating, while the bear market of sorrow can feel daunting. Emotional regulation isn't about eliminating downturns but managing them wisely. Both joy and sorrow are essential players in the emotional economy, contributing to a balanced and meaningful life.

When the bears arrive, it's important to avoid emotional "panic selling"—reacting impulsively to discomfort. Instead, take a step back, assess the situation, and make intentional choices that align with your emotional goals.

An emotional margin call occurs when your emotional debts outweigh your emotional assets—when stress, exhaustion, or overwhelm deplete your reserves. Emotional regulation helps you hedge against these moments, ensuring your portfolio remains robust even in challenging times.

Strategies include:

- **Diversification:** Spread your emotional energy across various aspects of life—work, relationships, hobbies, and self-care.

- **Regular Deposits:** Make small, consistent investments in activities that replenish you, like mindfulness, exercise, or meaningful conversations.

Some emotions are fleeting, like stocks that spike briefly before fading. Trying to hold onto them can be counterproductive. Emotional regulation teaches you to discern which feelings require immediate attention and which are worth a long-term investment.

For example:

- A fleeting irritation might not deserve significant energy.
- Deep gratitude, however, is worth holding onto and nurturing over time.

By recognizing the transient nature of some emotions, you free yourself from the pressure to overreact.

External influences—societal expectations, peer pressure, or cultural norms—can act like insider trading, dictating where you invest your emotional energy. True emotional wealth comes from aligning your trades with your authentic values, not with external pressures.

Ask yourself:

- Does this emotional investment align with who I am?
- Am I reacting to external trends, or am I staying true to my internal compass?

Just as financial diversification minimizes risk, emotional diversification ensures resilience. Don't put all your emotional eggs in one basket. Cultivate a range of emotional assets:

- **Joy:** Found in small pleasures and big victories.
- **Resilience:** Built through facing challenges head-on.
- **Love:** Shared with yourself and others.
- **Curiosity:** Fueling personal growth and exploration.

A well-diversified portfolio allows you to weather emotional downturns with grace and stability.

Think of emotional regulation as long-term financial planning for your inner self. What are your emotional goals for the future? Where do you want to be emotionally in five, ten, or twenty years?

Align your daily emotional choices with these aspirations. Small, consistent investments in emotional well-being today compound over time, creating a wealth of resilience and fulfillment in the years to come.

Your Emotional Dow Jones reflects the overall health of your inner portfolio. While fluctuations are inevitable, emotional regulation ensures your index remains stable over the long haul.

- **Celebrate Bull Markets:** Savor periods of positivity and flourishing emotions.
- **Prepare for Bear Markets:** Use emotional hedge funds—strategies like mindfulness, self-compassion, and support systems—to protect your assets during challenging times.

When you're ready to share new emotional aspects of yourself, think of it as launching an Emotional IPO (Initial Public Offering). Emotional regulation ensures you select the right emotions to share, at the right time, and with the right audience.

This cautious approach protects your emotional stock from crashing, ensuring that what you offer is met with respect and understanding.

Even the most skilled traders face setbacks. Emotional bankruptcy—a complete depletion of energy, motivation, or joy—is part of the journey. Emotional regulation helps you recover by:

- **Acknowledging the Loss:** Accepting the experience without self-judgment.
- **Rebuilding Slowly:** Reinvesting in small, meaningful ways to regain emotional wealth.
- **Learning from the Crash:** Identifying patterns that led to the downturn and adjusting your strategies accordingly.

Wise emotional investments pay dividends in the form of well-being, resilience, and self-awareness. These rewards are the fruits of consistent, intentional choices. Over time, they create a surplus of emotional wealth, enabling you to face life's challenges with strength and grace.

Key Takeaways

- **Embrace the Market Dynamics:** Recognize that emotional ups and downs are natural. Balance is achieved through mindful regulation.
- **Invest Wisely:** Focus on emotions that align with your values and long-term goals. Let go of those that drain your energy without adding value.
- **Diversify Your Portfolio:** Cultivate a variety of emotional assets to build resilience and adaptability.
- **Prepare for Fluctuations:** Use strategies like self-care and support systems to navigate emotional highs and lows.
- **Reap the Rewards:** Consistent emotional regulation leads to lasting well-being and inner peace.

Your emotional stock exchange is a dynamic and ever-evolving system. With thoughtful regulation and intentional investments, you can create a portfolio that thrives, even amidst life's uncertainties. Be the Warren Buffett of your emotional energy, and let your inner wealth grow steadily and sustainably. The market is yours—trade wisely.

Forging Your Own Path

Society hands us a script—worn, outdated, and all too familiar. It's a manual for blending into the comfortable, predictable backdrop of the status quo. Passed down through generations, this script dictates who we should be, how we should live, and what we should aspire to. But you weren't born to follow someone else's script. It's time to toss this tired narrative into the bonfire of rebellion and write a new story—your story—bold, unapologetic, and authentically yours.

The status quo hums like a well-rehearsed symphony, its melody predictable and safe. It hands out identical sheet music and demands conformity, punishing deviations with disapproving glances. But history's most extraordinary compositions are born from rebellion—where notes clash, dance, and create breathtaking new harmonies.

The world doesn't need another identical tune. It needs your unique rhythm, your daring improvisation, your fearless refusal to follow the conductor's baton.

Imagine a carnival where conformity is the star attraction. Matching clown costumes are mandatory, and individuality is banned. The loudspeakers blare: "Fit in or be cast out!" But somewhere within, you carry a different soundtrack—one that defies the monotony and demands to be played at full volume.

The carnival of conformity thrives on fear, but rebellion begins when you trade fear for freedom. Step out of the crowd, rip off the costume, and take center stage in your authentic attire, no matter how unconventional it might seem.

Deep within every soul lies a rebel waiting to break free. This is the part of you that longs to shrug off societal expectations, to challenge the norm, and to live unapologetically as yourself. Rebellion isn't about chaos for its own sake; it's about embracing the courage to be who you are, even when the world demands otherwise.

Let's dig deep into your rebel roots. Unearth the seeds of nonconformity and nourish them. They hold the potential to grow into a vibrant, unique existence that is yours alone.

There's a magnetic pull to rebellion—a call to leave behind the monotony of the status quo and venture into uncharted waters. The seas may be rough, but the treasures are worth the risk. Rebellion invites you to take that leap, to steer your ship toward authenticity, even when the destination is uncertain.

Answering the call of individuality means choosing to explore the unpaved paths of life, where every step is an act of creation, every misstep a lesson, and every discovery a victory.

From the moment we're born, invisible strings bind us to the expectations of others. These puppet strings guide our choices and movements, often without us even realizing it. But you are not a marionette.

It's time to take up the scissors of self-awareness and sever those strings. With each cut, you reclaim your autonomy, your choices, your life. Step into the spotlight not as a puppet but as the choreographer of your own dance.

The machinery of societal expectations is complex and relentless. But with the right tools, it can be dismantled. Enter the rebellion toolbox:

- **Wrenches of Authenticity:** Tighten your grip on your true self, refusing to let it slip under the weight of conformity.
- **Hammers of Self-Expression:** Smash through the barriers that stifle your individuality.
- **Screwdrivers of Unapologetic Individuality:** Remove the screws of societal pressure, one by one, until the entire structure collapses.

Tinker with the machinery until it grinds to a halt, and then use its pieces to build something uniquely yours.

On the other side of conformity lies liberation. Here, the air is thick with the scent of freedom, and the soil is fertile for authenticity. Breaking free from the status quo isn't just a rejection of norms; it's an invitation to discover who you truly are.

This journey of liberation is a path of self-discovery, an expedition into the uncharted territories of your being. It's here that you plant the seeds of a life that reflects your values, passions, and dreams.

The playbook society hands you is outdated—a relic of rules designed to maintain the status quo. Tear it up. Shred it. Let its remnants fuel the flames of your rebellion. In its absence, you're free to become the playwright of your own life.

Without a script, every moment becomes an opportunity to write a new chapter. Your story becomes a living testament to courage, creativity, and the refusal to settle for anything less than your truth.

Chaos isn't something to fear—it's something to embrace. In rebellion, chaos becomes a trusted companion, guiding you to unexpected discoveries and hidden strengths.

Picture yourself dancing through the chaos, missteps and all. Like salsa dancing through a hurricane, the unpredictability is wild, exhilarating, and utterly freeing. Each wrong turn becomes a new possibility, each stumble an opportunity to find your balance in the storm.

Defying normalcy is an art form, a deliberate act of creation that turns the mundane into a masterpiece. It's about painting outside the lines, adding bold colors where others see gray, and creating something extraordinary in a world that often celebrates the ordinary.

With every stroke of nonconformity, you redefine what's possible—not just for yourself, but for others who dare to watch and follow.

Remember, rebellion isn't just a mindset—it's a movement, a declaration of independence from the suffocating grasp of the status quo. It's a bold step into a world where individuality thrives, where creativity reigns, and where the ordinary is transformed into the extraordinary. In this chapter, we embrace the tools, symbols, and ethos of rebellion, turning our journey of nonconformity into a work of art.

Every rebellion has its symbols, and for a nonconformist, even the wardrobe becomes a canvas for self-expression. Say goodbye to the cookie-cutter uniformity of the status quo and welcome a collection of eclectic pieces that reflect your unique story.

Your rebellion wardrobe isn't about fashion trends; it's about authenticity. Each piece you wear—a bold scarf, mismatched socks, or an heirloom brooch—should be a statement of who you are. Strut through life as if the world were your runway, draped in the vibrant fabrics of individuality.

On the frontline of rebellion, fearlessness is your armor. This isn't the absence of fear but the courage to face it head-on, deflecting the arrows of judgment and criticism. Fearlessness is what allows you to stand tall amidst the doubters and naysayers, refusing to be silenced or diminished.

Victory in the battle against the status quo belongs to those who dare to stand out. With every step, you carve a path for others to follow, proving that authenticity is not just possible—it's powerful.

The status quo clings tightly to its unwritten rulebook, a set of rigid guidelines etched into the collective consciousness. These rules tell you who to be, how to act, and what to value. But these are not your rules.

Rebellion means writing your own manifesto—a declaration of authenticity, creativity, and individuality. Toss the status quo's rulebook into the flames and watch your personal manifesto ignite. In its fiery glow, you'll discover the freedom to live life on your terms.

Eccentricity is the heartbeat of nonconformity. It's the melody that fuels your rebellion, the rhythm that propels you forward. Embrace your quirks, your peculiarities, and the aspects of yourself that others may not understand.

To be eccentric is to be free—to march to your own beat, to sing your own song, to paint your own masterpiece. Let your rebellion be a celebration of the beautifully bizarre, a testament to the wonders of being unapologetically you.

Rebellion isn't just about breaking chains—it's about dismantling the norms that keep us confined. Every shattered expectation, every crumbled societal restriction, adds to the symphony of liberation.

This is a rebellion that resonates, each act of defiance echoing across the landscapes of conformity. With every broken chain, you reclaim a piece of yourself, and with every broken norm, you create space for something extraordinary to emerge.

Authenticity is the artist's palette of rebellion. Each bold brushstroke is a declaration of selfhood, a refusal to blend into the grayscale of societal expectations.

The canvas of your life is vast and waiting. Dip your brush into the vibrant hues of your true self and paint with wild abandon. Every stroke adds to the masterpiece of your rebellion, a testament to the beauty of living authentically.

Rebellion is more than a personal act—it's the catalyst for a cultural renaissance. When one person dares to defy the status quo, it inspires others to do the same. Together, these acts of courage create a ripple effect, ushering in a rebirth of creativity, individuality, and freedom.

This renaissance replaces the mundane with the extraordinary, transforming societal norms into a playground for innovation and self-expression. It's a revolution of the soul, where authenticity becomes the guiding light.

As a rebel, you are part of an unseen alliance—a coalition of nonconformists united by the desire to shatter the status quo. Though we may walk different paths, we amplify each other's voices, creating a chorus of rebellion that cannot be ignored.

Together, we form a force to be reckoned with. In the solidarity of this alliance, we find strength, inspiration, and the reassurance that we are not alone in our pursuit of authenticity.

Rebellion leaves an indelible mark. Its echoes linger, inspiring others to embark on their own journeys against conformity. These whispers of nonconformity are the legacy of your rebellion, a gift to those who come after you.

Your journey doesn't end with you. The ripples you create extend outward, touching lives you may never know, proving that one act of courage can spark countless others.

As you gaze toward the uncharted horizon of nonconformity, exhilaration courses through your veins. This is a frontier waiting to be explored, a boundless landscape where the compass of rebellion points you toward infinite possibilities.

With every step, you redefine what's possible. This is the essence of rebellion: not just rejecting the ordinary, but celebrating the extraordinary. The uncharted horizon beckons—will you answer its call?

Key Takeaways
- **Reject the Script:** The status quo thrives on predictability. Toss the playbook and write your own narrative.
- **Embrace Your Inner Rebel:** Rebellion isn't chaos for chaos's sake—it's the courage to live authentically.
- **Use Your Tools:** With authenticity, self-expression, and individuality, dismantle societal expectations piece by piece.
- **Liberation Awaits:** On the other side of conformity lies the freedom to discover and create your truest self.
- **Harness Fearlessness:** Use courage as your shield against judgment and ridicule, forging ahead with conviction.
- **Celebrate the Chaos:** Missteps and unpredictability are not failures—they're the path to creativity and growth.
- **Leave a Legacy:** The echoes of your rebellion inspire others to embark on their own journeys of self-discovery.

Rebellion is a journey of self-discovery, courage, and creation. It's not about defying for the sake of defiance—it's about daring to live authentically, to create boldly, and to inspire endlessly. As you forge your own path, remember: every step you take lights the way for others to follow. So, march forward, fearless and free, toward the uncharted horizon of possibility.

The Drumbeat You Can't Ignore

Life calls for boldness, for stepping into the arena adorned with the armor of self-expression and wielding the banner of authenticity. This is no place for half-measures. Raising your banner is a declaration of courage, a rallying cry to live unapologetically as your truest self. With bootstraps tightened and hearts fortified, the march toward self-expression begins.

Your banner is more than a symbol—it's a declaration. It doesn't conform to societal templates or expectations. It proclaims, "This is who I am." Each thread in its tapestry represents your individuality: the quirks that make you laugh, the passions that set your soul ablaze, and the scars that tell your stories of resilience.

This banner is not about perfection. It's about authenticity—a celebration of the messy, beautiful truth of who you are. As you raise it high, the drumbeat of your genuine self drowns out the noise of societal judgment, propelling you forward with every courageous step.

The battlefield of life is strewn with norms, expectations, and the weight of conformity. Charging into this chaos with your banner raised is an act of defiance. Each step becomes a thunderclap, shaking the foundations of societal constraints.

Authenticity doesn't blend in—it shatters the mold, turning the remnants of broken norms into the raw materials for creativity and freedom. Dancing amidst the debris of conformity, you embrace the chaos as a transformative force.

Your banner doubles as both shield and armor. It deflects the arrows of judgment and criticism, allowing you to stand tall despite life's inevitable wounds. Authenticity wears the armor of vulnerability—a paradox that reveals its true power.

Courage isn't about being untouchable; it's about standing firm in your truth even when exposed. Vulnerability disarms the superficial and empowers the genuine.

Adversity is inevitable, but your banner is battle-tested, a symbol of resilience. It stands firm in the winds of judgment, unwavering even in the face of life's fiercest storms. Each challenge strengthens its fabric, transforming it into an emblem of unshakable authenticity.

Before entering the battlefield, prepare with the war paint of self-love. This isn't arrogance but a declaration of your worthiness. Streaks of self-love across your face tell the world that you honor your individuality and that no external judgment can diminish your light.

Your banner isn't just a personal symbol; it's a beacon that attracts those who resonate with your authenticity. Together, you form a tribe—a collective bound by the shared commitment to genuine self-expression. Courage is amplified when it's shared, and authenticity becomes a shared language of connection.

At the top of your banner flies the pennant of imperfection. True authenticity embraces the quirks, scars, and unpolished edges that make you human. Flaws are not weaknesses but brushstrokes in the masterpiece of your individuality.

Raising your banner is not a one-time act; it's a lifelong exploration. Each step reveals new facets of your authentic self, peeling back layers of societal conditioning and self-doubt. Courage thrives in this continuous process of discovery.

The battlefield is not just a place of struggle—it's a crucible for growth and self-realization.

Your banner carries the horn of defiance, a clarion call to challenge the roles and masks society imposes. Authenticity is an act of rebellion, a refusal to accept a life confined by others' expectations. With every step, the horn blares louder, announcing your refusal to conform.

Above your banner shines the star of conviction, casting its light on the darkest corners of fear and self-doubt. Conviction illuminates the path of authenticity, ensuring that even in moments of uncertainty, the journey forward remains clear.

Belief in the worth of your authenticity fuels every stride, even when the path is rocky or steep.

When the day's battles subside, let your banner lead the victory march of self-approval. This triumph isn't about external validation but about the quiet assurance that you've honored your truest self. The reflection in the mirror becomes your greatest ally, the source of your deepest pride.

Each day, as your banner flutters in the winds of your journey, it adds a unique thread to the collective human tapestry. Your authenticity becomes a gift, inspiring others to raise their own banners and live courageously.

The legacy of your banner is one of transformation—a reminder that every act of genuine self-expression strengthens the larger narrative of humanity.

Key Takeaways
- **Claim Your Truth:** Your banner represents your individuality, woven from the traits and experiences that make you unique.
- **Defy Conformity:** Shatter societal norms with a battle cry of authenticity, turning judgment into fuel for growth.
- **Embrace Vulnerability:** Authenticity is strongest when paired with the courage to be vulnerable.
- **Foster Connection:** Your banner is a beacon that attracts kindred spirits, forming tribes of shared authenticity.
- **Leave a Legacy:** Every act of self-expression contributes to the larger tapestry of human courage and individuality.

Raising your banner is a bold act of self-assertion, a declaration that your true self is worthy of being seen and celebrated. By marching to the beat of your own drum, you inspire others to do the same, creating a world richer for its diversity and authenticity. Stand tall, fearless warrior, and let your banner fly high.

Week 3

Week 3 Action Plan: Deepening Authenticity and Embracing the Uncharted

Welcome to Week 3 of "Orchestrating Impact: Conducting Life's Symphony with Purpose and Resilience." This week, we focus on deepening our authenticity, embracing life's uncharted territories, and fostering resilience amidst life's unpredictability.

Day 1: "Where Every Voice is Heard"

- **Activity:** Host a small group discussion with friends or family, focusing on a topic where diverse opinions are encouraged. Practice active listening and ensure each voice is heard and valued.
- **Reflection:** How did this activity challenge or change your perspectives?

Day 2: "That Dissonant Note"

- **Activity:** Reflect on a recent experience that felt uncomfortable or challenging. Explore the lessons it offered and how it contributed to your growth.
- **Reflection:** What beauty or growth can you find in the discomfort of dissonant notes in your life?

Day 3: "Investing in Vintage Experiences"

- **Activity:** Identify one experience you've longed to invest in but have postponed or neglected—something that promises to enrich your life significantly, akin to a celestial gem. Commit to making this experience a reality, planning the first step you will take to bring this gem into your life's constellation.
- **Reflection:** Reflect on the celestial gem you've chosen to invest in. Why is this experience valuable to you, and how do you anticipate it will enrich your life?

Day 4: "Life Without Rose-Tinted Glasses"

- **Activity:** Spend the day consciously avoiding the tendency to romanticize or gloss over the more challenging aspects of your life. Face them head-on with honesty and courage.
- **Reflection:** How does embracing life's realities, without the rose-tinted glasses, alter your approach to challenges?

Day 5: "Blind to the Gems"

- **Activity:** Identify something or someone in your life you've taken for granted. Acknowledge its/his/her value and express gratitude in a meaningful way.
- **Reflection:** How does shifting your focus to the overlooked gems in your life change your feelings of gratitude and appreciation?

Day 6: "No Rehearsed Speeches"

- **Activity:** Engage in a conversation where you consciously avoid planning what to say next and be vulnerable and transparent. Allow the dialogue to flow naturally, responding authentically in the moment.
- **Reflection:** How does the absence of rehearsed speeches and daring to lead with your truest self, flaws and all affect the authenticity and depth of your conversations?

Day 7: Weekly Integration
- **Activity:** Review the week's activities and reflections. Create a piece of art (writing, painting, music) that represents your journey into deeper authenticity and embracing life's realities.
- **Reflection:** Reflect on your growth this week. How has embracing authenticity and life's uncharted territories enriched your experience?

This week's journey has been about embracing the full spectrum of life's experiences, learning to listen deeply, and celebrating the authenticity that each moment brings. As you prepare for Week 4, remember that each step taken is a step closer to conducting a life's symphony that resonates with the depth, balance, and resonance of your true self.

Where Every Voice is Heard

Life is not a monochrome canvas but a vivid explosion of colors, each representing a unique human experience. The richness of existence lies in this diversity—a kaleidoscope of individuality painting the grand masterpiece of humanity. Respect for diversity isn't just an ideal; it's the lens through which we view the beauty in our differences and the unity in our collective story.

Imagine life as a symphony, where every individual is a distinct note. Together, these notes form a melody of uniqueness—a harmonious blend of varied tones and rhythms that transcends time. Diversity doesn't create discord; it creates depth. Respect for diversity is the conductor's baton, ensuring every note is heard and every voice contributes to the masterpiece.

Each perspective enriches the symphony. Whether loud or soft, fast or slow, each adds its own resonance, creating movements that stir the soul.

Every human story is a thread in the vast tapestry of existence. Bold and vibrant threads catch the eye, while subtle, intricate ones provide balance and texture. The loom of respect for diversity weaves these threads into a fabric that tells the story of our shared humanity.

A tapestry without its full range of colors and patterns is incomplete. Respect ensures every thread, no matter how unconventional, finds its place and purpose.

Life resembles a mosaic—a collection of pieces, each shaped differently but essential to the larger picture. Every shard contributes to the intricate design, and respect for diversity is the glue that holds the mosaic together. Without it, the masterpiece would crumble, its beauty lost to fragmentation.

Each piece, no matter its size or color, is vital. Together, they create a vision far greater than the sum of its parts.

Picture humanity as a sprawling garden, brimming with flowers of every shape, size, and hue. Each bloom adds to the garden's beauty, offering a fragrance uniquely its own. Respect for diversity is the gardener's touch, tending to every plant, ensuring that all thrive.

The unconventional blooms, the ones that grow in unexpected places, often bring the greatest wonder. Their uniqueness inspires awe and reminds us of nature's boundless creativity.

Human cultures are not isolated; they are ingredients in a shared recipe of existence. Respect for diversity acts as the skilled chef, blending flavors to create a feast that delights every palate.

No single ingredient defines the dish. The interplay of tastes, textures, and aromas creates something far richer, where each element retains its essence while enhancing the whole.

Life's dance floor is expansive, inviting everyone to move to the rhythm of their own song. Respect for diversity ensures that no one is sidelined, fostering a celebration of styles, steps, and stories.

Every dancer adds something unique to the choreography. Together, the dance becomes a vibrant expression of humanity's collective creativity.

Picture a quilt made from countless patches, each representing a unique identity. Some are bold and colorful, while others are quiet and understated. Respect for diversity is the needle and thread, stitching these patches into a warm embrace that wraps around us all.

This quilt doesn't demand uniformity; it celebrates the individuality of each patch while creating unity in the larger design.

Life refracts through the prism of human experience, splitting into a spectrum of colors. Respect for diversity is the prism, allowing every perspective to shine.

Without the prism, light remains unbroken, its complexity unseen. Diversity reveals the full spectrum, dazzling us with its brilliance and teaching us the value of every hue.

At the intersection of identities, a complex terrain emerges. Race, gender, class, sexuality, and more weave a multidimensional tapestry. Respect for diversity is the cartographer's pen, charting these intersections and honoring the unique journeys that traverse them.

Understanding intersectionality ensures that no one's experience is overlooked. It highlights the interconnectedness of our struggles and triumphs.

Life is an open forum, where ideas—no matter how unconventional—find space to flourish. Respect for diversity is the moderator, maintaining a balance that ensures every voice contributes to the dialogue.

In this forum, differences aren't barriers; they are bridges. The exchange of thoughts strengthens understanding and deepens the collective wisdom.

Let the anthem of unity in diversity resound in your spirit. It's a melody of acceptance, a rhythm of understanding, and a chorus of belonging. Every voice matters, every story enriches, and every identity contributes to the symphony of humanity.

Standing tall in this kaleidoscope of significance means embracing the beauty of every individual. The dance of humanity is a shared celebration, where every step, note, and color adds to the brilliance of the whole.

Key Takeaways
- **Celebrate Individuality:** Each person adds a unique hue to the canvas of life. Respect for diversity ensures every color is cherished.
- **Create Harmony:** Diverse voices don't create discord—they create depth and richness in the symphony of humanity.
- **Weave Connections:** Every thread in humanity's tapestry matters. Respect ties them together into a unified whole.

- **Foster Belonging:** Diversity invites everyone to the table, ensuring no voice is left unheard or unseen.
- **Honor Intersectionality:** Understanding the intersections of identity ensures no perspective is excluded or marginalized.

The beauty of life lies in its diversity, where every voice, every story, and every experience contributes to the larger narrative of humanity. Respect for diversity isn't just about tolerance—it's about celebration, inclusion, and recognizing the profound strength found in our differences. Together, we create a world where every voice resonates and every soul is seen.

That Dissonant Note

In the wild ride we call life, a tempestuous, relentless, beautifully chaotic dance through the storms of adversity awaits. Life doesn't hand out neat invitations; it throws curveballs, derails plans, and challenges your every move. But here's the truth: the storm isn't here to break you—it's here to forge you.

This isn't a serene tea party of polite resilience; it's a gritty, unapologetic exploration of how to face life's storms with strength, humor, and an unyielding refusal to be beaten down. Strap on your boots, adjust your sails, and prepare to navigate the tumultuous waters of adversity like the resilient badass you are.

Adversity is the thunder in life's symphony, a dramatic overture that splits the sky and drenches you in challenges. It's loud, unrelenting, and impossible to ignore. But in this storm, resilience becomes your defiant anthem. You stand tall, not with umbrellas for protection, but with arms wide open, embracing the rain, daring the storm to do its worst.

This is the moment where the melody of resilience rises above the chaos, creating a harmony that turns life's dissonance into a symphony of strength.

Adversity crashes into your life like an uninvited guest—messy, disruptive, and utterly unwelcome. Picture it spilling wine on the pristine carpet of your carefully constructed plans. But instead of pushing it out the door, you pull up a chair, pour a drink, and say, "Alright, adversity, let's see what you've got."

Resilience isn't about avoiding the storm; it's about finding the rhythm within it. Dancing in the rain doesn't just defy the chaos—it transforms it into an opportunity for growth, laughter, and stories worth telling.

Adversity throws punches, but resilience is the fight in your gut—the refusal to back down. This isn't a dainty tap dance through challenges; it's a full-blown mosh pit, where you clash with adversity and emerge, bruised but unbroken. Resilience doesn't just endure the storm; it thrives in its midst.

Think of resilience as a rebellion against the tyranny of despair. It's the defiant middle finger raised to the universe's toughest challenges, a refusal to be crushed under the weight of hardship.

Life's story is full of plot twists that make you question everything. Adversity is the unexpected turn that upends your narrative, leaving you wondering what kind of lunatic is writing this script. But here's the twist within the twist: resilience flips the script.

You don't stop at frustration; you keep reading. The plot thickens, the challenges deepen, and you discover that adversity doesn't derail the story—it propels it. Each twist adds depth, character, and meaning to the narrative, making it one worth living.

Adversity hits hard, but resilience is the skillful counter. It's the jiu-jitsu move that uses adversity's momentum against itself. With precision and poise, resilience flips the script, turning obstacles into stepping stones.

Rather than shrinking from the fight, resilience embraces it, knowing that each grapple with adversity builds strength and wisdom. You don't just survive—you emerge victorious, with a grin that says, "Is that all you've got?"

Adversity often feels like the universe's cruel joke, catching you off guard and testing your patience. But resilience is the stand-up comedian who grabs the mic and turns the joke on its head.

Through resilience, tears turn into laughter, struggles into punchlines, and challenges into triumphs. Life's comedy isn't about avoiding the joke—it's about delivering it with such flair that even the universe has to applaud.

In the storm, adversity roars, but resilience responds with a rock anthem. It's the guitar solo that pierces through the chaos, reminding you that you're the headlining act in your life's story. This is your concert, and the challenges are just the opening act.

Grab your air guitar and shred through the chaos with unapologetic confidence. The storm isn't here to drown you; it's the backdrop for your greatest performance.

Adversity is relentless, like a boot camp designed to test your limits. It pushes, pulls, and demands everything you've got. Resilience, then, becomes the drill sergeant who transforms pain into power and struggle into strength.

Through adversity, you're not just enduring; you're training. Each challenge adds muscle to your spirit, each setback builds stamina, and each triumph proves that you're stronger than you thought. When life feels like boot camp, resilience ensures you leave it battle-hardened and ready for anything.

Adversity, for all its chaos and unpredictability, is the ultimate adventure. It throws unexpected twists, treacherous terrain, and cliffhangers your way, challenging you to navigate its labyrinth with grit and daring. But resilience? Resilience is the bold adventurer within, smirking at the storm, embracing the thrill, and forging ahead with relentless determination.

This journey is not about seeking the safety of well-trodden paths. It's about plunging into the unknown, ready for the unpredictable beauty of a life lived fully.

Adversity's valleys echo with challenges, but resilience responds with a roar. It's the rallying cry that shatters despair, the defiant proclamation that declares, "I will not yield."

This is no soft lullaby. Resilience is a battle hymn that stirs your inner strength and calls your spirit to arms. With each note, it rallies your courage, preparing you to not only face the fight but to win it.

Life's melody often encounters dissonant notes—moments where adversity threatens to derail the harmony. But resilience is the conductor, transforming discord into a triumphant crescendo.

Instead of resisting the disharmony, resilience embraces it, weaving it into the larger composition of your life. The result is a symphony of triumph, where even the darkest notes find their place in a masterpiece of perseverance.

Adversity feels like a relentless winter—harsh, cold, and unyielding. But resilience ushers in the spring, a season of renewal and growth. From the frozen ground of challenges bloom the flowers of strength, resilience, and wisdom.

Life's seasons may change, but resilience remains evergreen, standing tall through every storm. You don't simply endure the winter; you thrive in the spring it inevitably brings.

Adversity is the stomach-churning drop on life's rollercoaster, the twist that leaves you breathless. But resilience throws its hands in the air and laughs in the face of the chaos.

Rather than clinging to the safety bar with fear, resilience relishes the ride, finding joy in the exhilaration of the unpredictable. Every twist and turn becomes an opportunity to live fully, to embrace the adventure with a fearless heart.

The marks adversity leaves behind aren't wounds to hide—they're scars to wear proudly. Each one tells a story of survival, of battles fought and won.

Resilience doesn't conceal these scars; it celebrates them as badges of honor. They are the tangible evidence of your strength, the proof that you've faced the storm and emerged unbeaten.

Adversity is life's raw material—heavy, unwieldy, and seemingly unyielding. But resilience is the alchemist, transforming base challenges into the gold of opportunity.

Every obstacle becomes a stepping stone, every setback a chance to find hidden treasure. Resilience wields the alchemist's wand with grace, proving that even in the rubble, beauty and strength can be forged.

Adversity often feels like an oppressive regime, tightening its grip and dictating terms. Resilience rises as the rebellion, refusing to bow to the tyranny of despair.

It's an uprising of spirit, a fight for freedom from the chains of doubt and fear. With resilience unfurling its banner, you march forward, defiant and determined, turning the tide in your favor.

Adversity hands you a blank canvas, stark and intimidating. Resilience picks up the brush, creating a vibrant masterpiece out of the chaos.

Each stroke tells a story of survival, each hue reflects a moment of triumph. The result is not just art—it's a testament to the power of resilience, a visual symphony that captures the essence of your strength.

Adversity may set the race, but resilience takes the victory lap. It's the triumphant sprint to the finish line, arms raised in celebration of every challenge conquered.

This isn't a stumble across the line. Resilience powers you forward, propelling you with confidence and pride. Each step declares, "I faced adversity, and I triumphed."

Key Takeaways
- **Embrace the Storm:** Adversity isn't here to break you; it's here to forge you. Stand tall, arms wide, and dare the storm to bring its worst.
- **Dance Through the Chaos:** Find the rhythm within the storm. Turn adversity into an opportunity to grow, laugh, and live boldly.
- **Defy the Odds:** Resilience is the rebellion against despair, the defiance that refuses to be crushed by life's challenges.

- **Flip the Script:** Each plot twist is an invitation to deepen your story. Embrace the twists and discover their hidden gifts.
- **Rock Your Anthem:** Let resilience be the soundtrack to your challenges, a powerful reminder that you're the headlining act in your own life.

Adversity may test your mettle, but resilience proves your strength. With each challenge, you grow stronger, wiser, and more capable. The storm is not the end; it's the beginning of a story where you emerge victorious, painting a masterpiece of perseverance and running the race with unwavering courage. So, fellow adventurer, embrace the dissonant note and let resilience guide you to create a life that's nothing short of extraordinary.

Investing in Vintage Experiences

Life is a vast, cosmic attic cluttered with emotional debris and unnecessary baggage. Among the chaos, there are treasures—vintage experiences that hold meaning and enrich your soul. It's time to embark on a celestial journey to declutter, prioritize, and invest in moments that matter. Armed with your stardust broom, you'll sweep away irrelevance, making space for extraordinary memories and timeless experiences.

Picture your life as an overstuffed attic filled with forgotten boxes of misplaced priorities. Each box represents an emotional burden, a worry, or a care spent on things that don't spark joy. It's time to open these boxes, examine their contents, and toss what no longer serves you into the black hole of irrelevance.

Envision a cosmic vacuum cleaner—a black hole sucking up the clutter of outdated emotions, unnecessary anxieties, and misplaced obligations. As the clutter spirals into oblivion, it leaves behind a trail of stardust, illuminating the freedom that comes from letting go.

Think of yourself as the curator of your life's museum. Each exhibit should reflect the values, memories, and experiences that truly matter. With a discerning eye, you'll decide what deserves a place in your gallery and what belongs in the intergalactic dumpster fire of irrelevance.

Decluttering is not just about removal; it's about intentionality. Hold each emotional commitment and ask, "Does this enrich my life? Does it align with my values?" If the answer is no, cast it aside. What remains is a minimalist masterpiece—an emotional space where the extraordinary can flourish.

Setting boundaries is akin to placing astral stones in the cosmic landscape of your life. These markers delineate the space where your emotional energy is sacred, guarding it against the gravitational pull of distractions and unnecessary burdens.

Imagine your boundaries as a force field, repelling negativity and ensuring that only what truly matters can penetrate. Within this sanctuary, your emotional energy finds room to grow, nurturing the seeds of vintage experiences.

Once the clutter is gone, step into the vintage experience bazaar. Picture a bustling marketplace where the currency is meaningful moments and the rarest treasures are the ones that resonate with your soul.

Invest in the extraordinary: moments of joy, connection, and personal growth that grow more valuable with time. These are the experiences that become the stars in your galaxy, shining brightly and guiding your journey.

Envision a time-traveling carousel, each horse a vintage experience carrying you through cherished memories. With each spin, you relive the laughter, the lessons, and the love that have shaped your journey. This is the ride of a lifetime, fueled by intentional living and emotional investment.

Your emotional energy is a finite resource, much like a financial portfolio. Resilience becomes your advisor, guiding you to allocate this energy wisely. Diversify your investments: joy, peace, creativity, and connection. Watch as these investments grow, enriching your life and building a legacy of fulfillment.

In the landscape of your mind, cultivate a serene meditation garden filled with the beauty of vintage experiences. Picture this space as a retreat where you can pause, reflect, and rejuvenate. Each moment spent here reinforces your connection to what truly matters, grounding you in a sense of peace and purpose.

Imagine a world where everyone declutters their emotional space, choosing quality over quantity, depth over distraction. This is the movement of emotional minimalism, and you are at the forefront. By investing in vintage experiences and letting go of the irrelevant, you inspire others to do the same.

Your boundaries become a quasar—a radiant force that illuminates your inner strength and self-respect. Each decision to protect your emotional energy pulses with the power of intentional living, creating a beacon that others can see and emulate.

As you let go of unnecessary burdens, you give birth to a nebula of emotional freedom—a vibrant cloud of colors representing the liberation of your soul. Tend this nebula with care, ensuring it thrives as a testament to your commitment to live authentically and purposefully.

Every decision you make leaves a mark on the cosmic tapestry of your life. By investing in vintage experiences, you weave a legacy rich with meaning and beauty. This tapestry becomes a story of intentionality, a reminder that the journey is as important as the destination.

Key Takeaways

- **Declutter with Intention:** Let go of emotional baggage that no longer serves you, creating space for what truly matters.
- **Set Strong Boundaries:** Establish clear markers that protect your emotional energy and prioritize your well-being.
- **Invest in Meaningful Experiences:** Choose moments and memories that enrich your soul and grow more valuable over time.
- **Cultivate Emotional Freedom:** Build a life rooted in authenticity, purpose, and intentionality.
- **Leave a Legacy:** Weave a tapestry of meaningful experiences that tell the story of a life well-lived.

Life's true treasures aren't found in the clutter—they're discovered in the vintage experiences that resonate with your soul. By decluttering the unnecessary and investing in the extraordinary, you create a life that shines like a constellation in the vast cosmos of existence. So grab your stardust broom, dear traveler, and let the journey to emotional liberation begin.

Life Without Rose-Tinted Glasses

In the grittiest corner of self-help, the air is thick with realism and rose-tinted glasses are strictly prohibited. This isn't a space for perpetual sunshine or glitter-dusted platitudes. Instead, it's a sanctuary for unfiltered reality and honest reflection. Here, we embrace life's messiness with realistic optimism—a practical, compassionate approach to navigating chaos without sugarcoating it.

Life isn't a neatly tied package adorned with perfect ribbons. It's a tangle of frayed edges, mismatched wrapping paper, and unexpected surprises. Peeling back the layers reveals the raw, unfiltered reality lurking beneath.

Realistic optimism begins with this acknowledgment: life is messy. But within that mess lies the beauty of growth, resilience, and authenticity. Confronting the chaos doesn't mean we reject joy; it means we embrace the entire spectrum of human experience.

Imagine life as a symphony, but instead of a perfectly composed melody, it's a chaotic cacophony of highs, lows, and dissonant notes. Realistic optimism doesn't cover its ears or tune out the discord. Instead, it picks up the conductor's baton, weaving those unexpected notes into a masterpiece.

The goal isn't to eliminate chaos but to find harmony within it. Each note—whether joyful, sorrowful, or bittersweet—adds depth and richness to the symphony of existence.

The world often drowns us in relentless positivity, promising perpetual bliss as the ultimate goal. But this glittery facade ignores the reality of hardship, struggle, and imperfection.

Realistic optimism is the immune response to this positivity pandemic. It replaces toxic positivity with a grounded perspective, one that values authenticity over superficial cheerfulness. Instead of covering life's messiness with sparkles, we face it head-on, discovering meaning in the chaos.

In the philosophy of realistic optimism, chaos isn't an enemy to be vanquished but a dance partner to be embraced. The Zen of chaos teaches us to find serenity within life's unpredictability, to move with the currents rather than against them.

Life's dumpster fires don't need to be extinguished immediately. Sometimes, they offer warmth, light, or even a chance to roast marshmallows. The key is learning to adapt, finding the moments of joy and camaraderie amidst the mess.

The cracks and flaws in our lives are not blemishes to be hidden but fingerprints of authenticity. Like the Japanese art of kintsugi, where broken pottery is repaired with gold, realistic optimism transforms imperfections into sources of beauty.

Rather than striving for an unattainable ideal, we learn to appreciate the flawed, raw, and genuine elements of our existence.

Resilience isn't about bouncing back with effortless grace. It's about stumbling, struggling, and slowly finding your footing after life knocks you down. Realistic optimism acknowledges that some setbacks leave deep potholes, and the road to recovery is rarely linear.

In the gym of reality, resilience is the personal trainer urging us to lift life's heavy weights—not for perfection, but for strength. It's about showing up, even when the dumbbells feel impossibly heavy.

Life's picture is incomplete, its pieces scattered and mismatched. Some may never be found. Realistic optimism doesn't promise a perfect puzzle but teaches us to find beauty in what we can piece together.

The missing pieces don't diminish the masterpiece; they add intrigue, inviting us to imagine and appreciate the picture's uniqueness.

Realistic optimism extends a compassionate hand to our imperfect selves. It doesn't demand flawless performance or perpetual progress. Instead, it offers a gentle hug after failure, a kind word in moments of doubt.

This isn't about self-improvement through harsh critique but self-acceptance through understanding. Compassion meets realism on life's canvas, creating a picture that celebrates effort over outcome.

Life's soundtrack isn't a one-note tune. It's a bittersweet symphony, where the minor chords of struggle enhance the resonance of the major chords of triumph. Realistic optimism teaches us to appreciate the full melody, savoring the highs without denying the lows.

The depth of our experience comes not from avoiding pain but from weaving it into the fabric of our story.

When we look into the unfiltered mirror of realistic optimism, we see life as it truly is—messy, chaotic, and beautifully imperfect. We don't turn away or cover the cracks with glitter. Instead, we honor the reflection, finding strength in its raw authenticity.

This mirror doesn't flatter or deceive. It reveals, teaching us to accept ourselves and our journey with open eyes and resilient hearts.

Key Takeaways
- **Face the Mess:** Life is messy, chaotic, and unpredictable. Embracing this reality is the first step toward realistic optimism.
- **Find Harmony in Chaos:** Don't fear the dissonance. Learn to conduct life's symphony, turning chaos into a masterpiece.
- **Reject Toxic Positivity:** True optimism isn't about denying struggles; it's about finding meaning and resilience within them.
- **Celebrate Imperfection:** Life's cracks and flaws are marks of authenticity and beauty. Appreciate them as part of your unique story.
- **Extend Compassion:** Realistic optimism is rooted in self-compassion, valuing effort and authenticity over perfection.

Realistic optimism isn't about chasing an unattainable ideal or hiding from life's struggles. It's about embracing the full, messy spectrum of existence with courage and grace. By peeling off the rose-tinted glasses, we see life in all its vivid complexity—and discover the strength and beauty in its imperfections.

Blind to the Gems

Life's opportunities are not confined to the shallow waters of scarcity thinking. They lie in the vast, uncharted depths of an abundance mindset. This isn't about surface-level optimism or hollow affirmations. It's a profound dive into the richness of possibilities, a journey where limitations dissolve, and the treasure of untapped potential awaits discovery.

Put on your diving gear and leave the kiddie pool behind—it's time to explore the ocean of abundance with curiosity, courage, and clarity.

Scarcity thinking is a mental abyss, a Bermuda Triangle where dreams vanish, and potential is left adrift. It whispers lies of "not enough"—not enough time, resources, talent, or opportunity. It keeps you navigating with a leaky dinghy, constantly bailing water instead of charting a course to growth.

Breaking free from scarcity requires a mindset shift. Imagine trading that dinghy for a sleek, unsinkable vessel—the abundance mindset. With it, you can cut through the waves, chart new courses, and embrace the vastness of possibility.

Scarcity waters are teeming with pirates of limitation, ready to plunder your aspirations and leave you clinging to scraps of what could have been. But you are not defenseless. Raise the Jolly Roger of abundance and take back control.

Abundance thinking isn't passive; it's a bold declaration that you refuse to live confined by fear or lack. This mindset equips you to repel self-doubt and embrace your potential with confidence.

In the treasure chest of abundance, gratitude is the map leading to untold riches. Scarcity thinkers overlook the gems scattered in their daily lives, too focused on what they lack to see the treasures they already possess.

Abundance thinkers pause to recognize and appreciate these gifts. Each moment of gratitude uncovers another jewel—an opportunity, a connection, a lesson—that adds to the wealth of their lives.

Opportunities are the coral reefs of abundance, vibrant ecosystems brimming with life and potential. Scarcity thinkers fear entanglement, avoiding the reefs and missing out on their treasures. Abundance thinkers, however, dive in with curiosity, exploring every nook and cranny for growth and discovery.

Each twist and turn holds the promise of something new—if only you're willing to dive deeper.

Scarcity clings to the idea that giving depletes your resources, but abundance recognizes that generosity is regenerative. Like sonar guiding a pod of dolphins, generosity sends out waves of positivity, attracting opportunities and relationships in return.

The more you share—be it time, wisdom, or kindness—the richer your life becomes.

Adversity can shipwreck the unprepared, but for those with an abundance mindset, resilience is the rising tide that lifts their ship above the storm.

Scarcity sees setbacks as insurmountable. Abundance views them as waves to ride, knowing that every ebb is followed by a flow, every storm by calm waters.

Scarcity keeps you floating in the shallows, afraid to venture into the unknown. Abundance equips you with creativity—a submarine capable of exploring the depths of possibility.

Beneath the surface lies uncharted potential. Abundance thinkers embrace the unknown, uncovering hidden wonders and crafting solutions that scarcity thinking would never dare to imagine.

Fear lurks in scarcity's waters, a leviathan that feeds on self-doubt and hesitation. Abundance thinkers don't pretend it isn't there. They face it head-on, transforming its presence into a compass pointing toward uncharted territories.

Each encounter with fear becomes an opportunity to grow braver, stronger, and more attuned to the vastness of their own potential.

In the murky waters of doubt, self-belief becomes bioluminescence—a light that cuts through the darkness. Scarcity thinkers are paralyzed by shadows; abundance thinkers shine from within, guiding themselves through uncertainty with the glow of confidence.

This inner light doesn't extinguish in adversity. Instead, it grows brighter, illuminating paths unseen by those bound by scarcity.

Without direction, even the most powerful ship will drift aimlessly. Scarcity thinkers let the currents carry them wherever they please. Abundance thinkers set their course by the North Star of purpose, steering with intention and clarity.

Purpose transforms the journey from aimless wandering into a meaningful expedition, where each decision aligns with a greater vision.

Mindfulness anchors the abundance mindset, keeping you present and aware as you sail through life's waters. Scarcity thinkers are blind to the ripples, colliding with obstacles they never saw coming. Abundance thinkers, attuned to every wave, navigate with precision and grace.

Through mindfulness, abundance thinkers avoid the rocks of anxiety, steering their ship with calm and confidence.

At the end of this deep-sea journey lies a profound truth: abundance isn't about accumulating wealth or possessions. It's about creating a legacy rich with meaningful experiences, connections, and contributions.

Each treasure discovered, each wave ridden, each scar earned adds to the tapestry of a life lived fully. The gems of abundance shine not just for you but for those who sail alongside you, inspired by your courage to venture beyond the shallows.

Key Takeaways

- **Transform Your Mindset:** Scarcity keeps you adrift; abundance empowers you to chart new courses and embrace life's vastness.
- **Recognize the Gems Around You:** Gratitude uncovers the treasures hiding in plain sight.
- **Dive Deep into Opportunity:** The coral reefs of life's potential await those brave enough to explore beyond the surface.
- **Harness the Power of Generosity:** Sharing your resources creates ripples of abundance that return tenfold.
- **Navigate with Purpose:** Let your vision and values guide you like the North Star through life's uncertainties.

Beyond the shallows lies a world of infinite possibilities. The abundance mindset invites you to dive deep, to discover the gems hidden in the depths, and to navigate life with courage, creativity, and purpose. The ocean of life is vast, but your potential is boundless—so set sail and embrace the horizon of abundance.

No Rehearsed Speeches

The dance floor of authenticity is calling—a space where raw emotions, unfiltered thoughts, and unapologetic self-expression take center stage. This isn't about perfect choreography or rehearsed routines. It's about moving freely to your own rhythm, tossing conformity aside, and stepping boldly into the spotlight of your true self.

Authenticity is not a performance; it's a ballad sung straight from the soul. It's not about rehearsing lines for an invisible audience but about letting your voice echo with honesty. When you dance to the tune of your authentic self, there's no need for approval—your moves are enough.

Picture this as your moment to throw open the doors, waltz onto the floor, and groove unapologetically to your own melody.

Vulnerability and authenticity are partners in a daring tango. This isn't a dance of perfection but one of exposed hearts and unguarded truths. In this dance, each step celebrates your imperfections, and each turn reminds you that true connection happens when you dare to lead with your raw, unfiltered self.

Authenticity thrives in transparency, spinning the truth on its head and letting it shine for all to see. There's no smoke, no mirrors—just the gritty beauty of your story, bruises and all. The Breakdance of Transparency isn't about hiding flaws; it's about showing the world that your scars tell a story worth celebrating.

Imagine a waltz where your thoughts flow freely, unencumbered by societal filters or expectations. This isn't about rehearsed speeches or canned responses—it's about the sway of spontaneous ideas, each one a step closer to the rhythm of your authentic voice.

Life's dance floor is no place for poker faces. The Salsa of Genuine Emotions invites you to move to the rhythm of real feelings. Sway with joy, twirl with passion, and stomp through the storms of sadness. Authenticity means letting every emotion find its place in the dance.

Radical acceptance is the beat of authenticity, a freestyle groove that embraces every quirk, scar, and imperfection. This isn't about judging yourself—it's about creating a life where all the pieces, even the messy ones, contribute to the beauty of the dance.

Authenticity and integrity glide hand in hand across life's stage. With each step, you honor your values, moving gracefully through challenges without compromising who you are. The Electric Slide of Integrity lights up the floor, ensuring your principles shine brightly through every move.

Authenticity builds bridges. It's the dance of honest conversations and unmasked interactions. In the Foxtrot of True Connections, every step deepens bonds, creating relationships that stand firm through the rhythm of life's highs and lows.

Purpose is the groove that guides authenticity, a melody that sways with intention. In the Reggae of Soulful Purpose, you find your life's rhythm, dancing toward goals that resonate deeply with your heart. This isn't just a song; it's an anthem of meaning.

Authenticity isn't a solo act. It's a duet with compassion, a ballet where you glide gracefully through differences, understanding others while staying true to yourself. In this dance, empathy creates harmony, weaving a choreography of connection and respect.

Challenges may shake the dance floor, but authenticity performs the Charleston of Resilience, spinning adversity into strength. Each move defies setbacks, proving that even when the rhythm falters, the dance goes on.

Growth is a slow, steady rhythm—an intimate rumba with change. Authenticity means embracing the dance of transformation, twirling with new experiences, and letting the music of growth guide you toward becoming your truest self.

Authenticity doesn't sit quietly in the corner. It's a headbanging, boundary-breaking Rock 'n' Roll rebellion against conformity. This dance demands boldness, urging you to stomp on the status quo and create an encore performance that's entirely your own.

Key Takeaways

- **Move to Your Rhythm:** Authenticity isn't a choreographed routine—it's an unscripted, genuine dance to the beat of your soul.

- **Embrace Vulnerability:** True connection happens when you step onto the floor with an unguarded heart.
- **Build True Connections:** Authenticity strengthens relationships by fostering honest, unmasked interactions.
- **Grow with Grace:** The dance of life is ever-changing. Authenticity means adapting to the music of growth and transformation.
- **Rebel with Confidence:** Don't fear breaking the mold. Authenticity thrives in rebellion, challenging norms and celebrating individuality.

Let the spotlight find you as you take the stage of authenticity. Dance with passion, vulnerability, and purpose. In the end, the most beautiful choreography is the one created by living unapologetically, swaying to the rhythm of your unique self, and inspiring others to find their own beat.

Week 4

Week 4 Action Plan: Embracing Your Unique Journey and Mastering Balance

Welcome to the final week of "Orchestrating Impact: Conducting Life's Symphony with Purpose and Resilience." This week, we focus on celebrating your unique journey, mastering the balance in life's complexities, and solidifying the lessons learned for lasting impact.

Day 1: "The Humble Reminder"

- **Activity:** Identify a recent setback or failure you've encountered. Reflect on the journey that led there, acknowledging where you started, the progress and growth you experienced, and the lessons learned. Recognize and honor the journey, not just the endpoint.
- **Reflection:** Consider the value of this setback as a "humble reminder". Reflect on how acknowledging and learning from our failures can help maintain a grounded perspective and foster gratitude for the journey, regardless of its ups and downs. How does embracing these humble reminders contribute to your personal growth and resilience?

Day 2: "It Glitters Like the Sun"

- **Activity:** Consciously confront your Fear Of Missing Out (FOMO) for the entire day. Whenever you feel the tug of FOMO—perhaps when seeing social media posts or hearing about events you're not attending—acknowledge it, then redirect your focus to the value of your current activities or the choice to enjoy solitude or different company.
- **Reflection:** Reflect on your experience. How did recognizing and standing up to FOMO change your perspective on your day's activities? Did this exercise reveal any deeper insights about what truly matters to you, beyond social trends or the fear of missing out? How can you apply this awareness to cultivate more meaningful, distraction-free moments in your life?

Day 3: "Courageous Self-Expression"

- **Activity:** Do something that requires you to express yourself courageously, whether it's sharing your art, speaking your truth, or standing up for your beliefs.
- **Reflection:** Reflect on the power of courageous self-expression. How does it feel to share your true self with the world?

Day 4: "The Wild, Unrestrained Extravaganza of Life"

- **Activity:** Actively seek out opportunities to perform acts of kindness, big or small, for the entire day. Whether it's complimenting a stranger, volunteering your time, or simply offering a helping hand, let generosity guide your actions.
- **Reflection:** Reflect on your day of deliberate generosity. How did engaging in selfless acts alter the rhythm of your daily routine? Did you notice a shift in your own energy or mood? Consider how these moments of generosity resonate with your core values and enhance your life's melody. How can incorporating regular acts of kindness into your life transform the way you navigate your personal "dance floor"?

Day 5: "Not Your Grandma's Library"
- **Activity:** Explore a new book, podcast, or documentary on a topic outside your usual interests. Expand your horizons and knowledge base.
- **Reflection:** How does diversifying your sources of knowledge and inspiration influence your perspective on life?

Day 6: "The Oracle Within"
- **Activity:** Spend quiet time in reflection or meditation, seeking the guidance of your inner oracle. Bring to mind a situation or decision that's been weighing on you. Instead of analyzing it with logic alone, close your eyes, take deep breaths, and ask your inner oracle for guidance. Pay attention to the first feeling, image, or thought that arises, even if it seems unconnected. Jot it down if it helps you focus.
- **Reflection:** Reflect on the insight you received during your moment with your inner oracle. Was the guidance surprising, or did it affirm what you already felt? Consider the difference between this intuitive insight and your rational thoughts on the matter. How can integrating this intuitive wisdom enrich your decision-making process and enhance your journey forward?

Day 7: Weekly Integration and Balance Mastery
- **Activity:** Create a balance wheel for your life, dividing it into segments that represent different areas (work, relationships, personal growth, health). Assess and plan how to balance these areas moving forward.
- **Reflection:** Reflect on the journey through this book and the past four weeks. How have the insights and activities helped you master the balance in your life?

This week's journey marks the culmination of your exploration into harmony, balance, and resonance within life's symphony. As you move forward, remember the lessons learned, the growth experienced, and the resilience built. Your ability to orchestrate impact, navigate chaos, and cultivate depth in your life's symphony will continue to grow as you apply these principles daily. Carry forward the courage, wisdom, and authenticity you've nurtured, and let them guide you in conducting a life of meaningful impact and resilient harmony.

The Humble Reminder

We're declaring independence from the paralyzing grip of the fear of failure. This isn't just about sidestepping fear—it's about transforming it into your ally, turning failure into fertile ground for growth, and embracing the truth that the journey is just as meaningful as the destination.

Failure isn't your enemy; it's the wise companion that challenges, teaches, and propels you forward. Let it guide you, not intimidate you.

Failure often feels like a harsh spotlight, but in reality, the light shines brightest on those who dare to act, stumble, and rise again. The critics may watch, but you're the one with the courage to try. Your efforts—and the lessons learned—are what matter.

The fear of failure stems from a fixation on perfection and pre-written success stories. Break free from that narrative. Your journey is a one-of-a-kind masterpiece, filled with unexpected twists, setbacks, and triumphs that only you can experience.

Failure is an honest mirror reflecting areas for growth. It doesn't distort; it clarifies. Each stumble reveals what you need to strengthen and refine. Looking into this mirror is an act of courage, one that sets the stage for genuine improvement.

Imagine failure as a note in the symphony of resilience. It's not the finale; it's the pause that transitions into a powerful new movement. Resilience is the melody that turns those notes into something extraordinary.

The fear of failure traps you in a padded cell disguised as a comfort zone. But life isn't meant to be lived in confinement. It's an adventure that calls for risk, exploration, and bold leaps into the unknown.

Think of failure as tuition in the university of life. Yes, the cost is high—pride, effort, and sometimes pain—but the lessons are invaluable. Those who graduate from this university wear their scars as badges of honor, proof of their journey toward wisdom.

Fear of failure convinces you to aim low, to settle for mediocrity. But mediocrity is a cage. The true magic lies in aiming for the extraordinary, knowing that even if you miss, you'll land somewhere remarkable.

Failure is the fertile soil where creativity and innovation take root. Every misstep becomes a seed, germinating ideas and paths you wouldn't have otherwise explored.

The illusion of perfection is one of the most persistent lies fear tells. Life isn't flawless—it's messy, unpredictable, and gloriously imperfect. Accepting this truth liberates you to embrace your journey, flaws and all, without apology.

Picture yourself as a tightrope walker. Fear of failure might make you hesitate, trembling with doubt. But true growth comes when you step forward, arms wide, and embrace the thrilling dance between success and failure.

Fear of failure is a prison we build ourselves. But the keys to freedom are always within reach. When you embrace failure as part of the process, the doors swing open, and you step into the vast world of possibility.

The doubts of others often echo in our fear of failure. Silence that noise. Let your inner voice of courage drown out those echoes as you carve your path with boldness and conviction.

Failure is the canvas where your character is painted. Each setback adds depth, texture, and resilience, creating a masterpiece uniquely yours. The vibrant hues of perseverance and strength are visible only when you allow yourself to stumble and rise again.

As the architect of your dreams, fear of failure might make you hesitate, questioning every move. But hesitation won't build the life you want. Seize the blueprints of your aspirations, build the grand structures you envision, and let failure serve as the scaffolding that holds your dreams aloft.

Failure is a humble reminder of your humanity. It's not a flaw but a testament to your willingness to try, to venture beyond the safety of the familiar. It's a badge of courage that says, "I dared to dream."

The unknown, so often feared, is where the magic happens. Rather than fearing it, embrace it. The unknown is the blank canvas where the most vivid, exhilarating adventures are painted.

Failure isn't the end; it's the spark for a new beginning. Each time you rise, stronger and wiser, you inspire others and defy the odds. Let your journey be a testament to the power of resilience, the beauty of imperfection, and the triumph of the human spirit.

Key Takeaways

- **Failure is a Teacher:** Every stumble reveals valuable lessons. Embrace failure as a mirror that reflects growth opportunities.
- **Dare Greatly:** The spotlight shines on those bold enough to try. Let others watch as you navigate your unique, unscripted journey.
- **Redefine Perfection:** Life's beauty lies in its imperfections. Shed the illusion of flawlessness and embrace your authentic self.
- **Break Free from Fear:** Fear of failure is a prison of your own making. Embrace failure, and you unlock the doors to liberation.
- **Turn Failure into Fertile Ground:** Every setback is an opportunity to plant seeds of creativity, resilience, and transformation.

The journey is what matters. Each failure is a chapter in your story, a note in your symphony, and a brushstroke on your canvas. With every stumble, you grow stronger, and with every rise, you inspire. Let fear know it has met its match. You are the author of your life, the conductor of your symphony, and the architect of your dreams. Keep going—the odyssey is far from over.

It Glitters Like the Sun

Distractions glitter in the sun, dazzling and deceptive, tempting you to veer off course. They are the sirens of the modern age, singing songs of immediate gratification and pulling even the most resolute sailor toward the rocky shores of procrastination. Yet, the adaptable sailor knows how to navigate these treacherous waters—plugging their ears to the melody and steering their ship toward purpose.

Picture distractions as the Bermuda Triangle of productivity. Entering their domain without preparation can lead to the disappearance of your time, energy, and focus without a trace. However, the adaptable sailor is not helpless. Armed with a clear map of priorities and the wisdom to discern their true course, they chart a path that keeps their journey intact, avoiding the traps that claim so many.

Distractions, like cunning pirates, board your ship unnoticed, stealing the treasures of time and focus. They operate silently, often disguised as harmless moments of leisure or productivity. But the adaptable sailor is prepared—ready to fire a well-aimed cannonball of intentional focus to fend off these marauders and protect the cargo of their goals.

In the digital age, distractions take the form of incessant notifications, social media rabbit holes, and the never-ending allure of streaming content. These are the digital sirens of our time. The adaptable sailor, firm at the helm of their smartphone and computer, resists their call. Instead, they navigate with deliberate actions, choosing apps and technologies that align with their purpose rather than succumbing to the virtual abyss.

Multitasking masquerades as a productivity hack, but it often results in a chaotic jumble of unfinished tasks. It is the frenzied dance of distractions, promising efficiency but delivering disorder. The adaptable sailor, wise to this deception, opts for the deliberate waltz of single-tasking. With each step, they move closer to their goals, unhurried and unbothered by the frenetic pace around them.

Fear of Missing Out (FOMO) is one of distraction's most persuasive whispers. It tugs at your anchor, urging you to chase every fleeting trend or opportunity. But the adaptable sailor understands the power of saying "no." Anchored by their priorities, they steer clear of unnecessary detours, trusting that their chosen path will lead to deeper fulfillment.

Distractions often disguise themselves as urgent tasks, demanding immediate attention. But urgency is a clever trickster, and not every ripple in the waters warrants a course correction.

The adaptable sailor discerns between genuine storms and passing winds, keeping their focus on what truly matters.

Imagine your focus as a symphony, where each instrument plays a vital role in creating a harmonious masterpiece. Distractions are the discordant notes, jarring and disruptive. The adaptable sailor acts as the conductor, ensuring that these off-key interruptions are silenced, allowing the symphony of focus to unfold with grace and intention.

Distractions create a labyrinth of choices, each path seemingly as enticing as the next. Without direction, it's easy to wander aimlessly, wasting time in a futile search for progress. The adaptable sailor wields a mental compass, staying true to their purpose and slicing through the maze with clarity and precision.

Distractions are like mischievous winds, threatening to blow you off course. But even these can be harnessed. The adaptable sailor adjusts their sails, turning potential setbacks into opportunities for momentum. By reframing distractions as moments for recalibration, they stay in control of their ship's trajectory.

Some distractions appear as mirage islands, offering the promise of rest or reward. Yet upon closer inspection, these diversions often lead to wasted time rather than replenishment. The adaptable sailor recognizes these illusions for what they are and presses forward, keeping their sights on the true landmarks of their journey.

Distractions are the quicksand of productivity, subtle and slow in their pull. They masquerade as harmless indulgences, yet over time, they consume your momentum. The adaptable sailor avoids these traps with a lifeline of discipline, choosing deliberate action over fleeting pleasure.

The fight against distractions is not one to be avoided but embraced. Think of it as a battlefield where your focus is the warrior, wielding the sword of resilience. Each choice to stay the course is a victory against the forces that would rob you of your potential.

Not all distractions are inherently negative. Some, like shooting stars, are fleeting and beautiful, offering brief moments of inspiration. The adaptable sailor, with their eyes fixed on the constellations of long-term goals, appreciates these moments without being led astray.

The sea of distractions is vast and unpredictable, but the adaptable sailor is steadfast, equipped with purpose as their compass, resilience as their sail, and clarity as their anchor. With these tools, they chart a deliberate course, turning obstacles into opportunities and ensuring their journey is one of meaning and mastery.

Stay vigilant, fellow sailor. In the mastery of adaptability lies the key to navigating the glittering but perilous waters of modern life. Keep your gaze on the horizon, and let purpose guide you through the tides.

Key Takeaways
- **Focus is a Lifeline:** Distractions are tempting, but focus is your anchor, keeping you steady amidst the chaos.
- **Prioritize with Purpose:** Use your map of priorities to navigate life's demands and avoid being pulled off course.
- **Adapt and Conquer:** Like a skilled sailor, learn to adjust your sails to steer through distractions with intention.

- **Beware of Illusions:** Distractions often masquerade as urgency; discern between what truly matters and what doesn't.
- **Purpose as Your Compass:** Keep your eyes on your long-term goals to avoid being derailed by short-term temptations.

Courageous Self-Expression

Courageous self-expression is the anthem of living authentically, a bold declaration that your life is your own canvas. It is not about following someone else's blueprint but about daring to create your own—one vibrant, unapologetic stroke at a time. Let us explore the fearless art of embracing your true self.

Imagine holding the sledgehammer of authenticity, poised to break apart the fragile, outdated expectations that surround you. These societal norms, like delicate china, may seem untouchable, but they only hold power if left unchallenged. Courageous self-expression is your act of redecorating—not with the predictable, generic patterns handed to you but with bold, handcrafted pieces that reflect your unique spirit.

Society often hands us a one-size-fits-all manual for life, complete with step-by-step instructions on how to build an existence that fits neatly within its cookie-cutter mold. This is the IKEA Syndrome, a condition that trades individuality for conformity. But life is not mass-produced. True living is a DIY project, and you are the artisan. Courageous self-expression means tossing out the prefab blueprints and crafting a life that resonates with your soul—complete with secret passages, trapdoors, and walls painted in the vivid colors of your imagination.

If life is a symphony, societal expectations are the dissonant notes threatening to disrupt the melody. Courageous self-expression is the conductor's wand, orchestrating a masterpiece that aligns with your authentic rhythm. Each decision, each action, becomes part of a harmonious composition that earns a standing ovation—not from others, but from yourself.

Picture societal expectations as an imposing fortress, its walls designed to keep you contained. Courageous self-expression is the battering ram, breaking through the barriers that confine your individuality. As the walls crumble, sunlight pours into the space where your authentic self can flourish. This is not a rebellion for its own sake but a liberation of the real you, hidden beneath layers of "shoulds" and "musts."

Imagine societal expectations as kindling for a fire. Into the blaze, you throw the scripts and rulebooks that have dictated your life—the prescribed roles, the arbitrary benchmarks, the hollow metrics of success. Courageous self-expression is the fuel that transforms this bonfire into an inferno of liberation. Watch as the flames consume the chains of conformity, leaving only the clarity of who you are and what truly matters.

Courageous self-expression is a banner raised high in the march against conformity. It's a declaration that your life is not a paint-by-numbers exercise. Instead, you wield the brush of individuality with fearless strokes, creating a masterpiece that may be messy and unpredictable but is unmistakably yours. Each flag on this march represents a unique story, a testament to the beauty of diversity and the power of authenticity.

Societal expectations often feel like a labyrinth, full of dead ends and suffocating walls. Courageous self-expression is your machete, carving a path through the tangle of "supposed to" and "ought to." Each step forward is a triumph of self-definition, leading you into the open field of possibility and freedom.

Consider your life a garden and societal norms the barren soil that resists growth. Courageous self-expression is the act of guerrilla gardening, planting seeds of individuality where none are expected. As these seeds grow, they transform the desolation into a riot of color—each bloom a celebration of your authentic choices.

Life's runway belongs to you. Forget off-the-rack expectations; this is your couture show. Draped in the fabrics of audacity, you strut with confidence, designing your own wardrobe of experiences and values. Courageous self-expression is the applause that follows—not from the crowd, but from the deepest parts of your soul.

Courageous self-expression is graffiti sprayed across the gray walls of societal norms. Each bold stroke of color reclaims space, turning the cityscape of conformity into a vibrant canvas of individuality. This art is not for approval—it's a reminder to yourself and others that the world is meant to be lived in your colors.

Picture courageous self-expression as a thunderstorm breaking the oppressive heat of expectations. Lightning strikes illuminate the truth of who you are, and the rain washes away the residue of conformity. When the storm passes, what remains is the cleansed, fertile ground where you can grow freely.

From the ashes of societal expectations rises the phoenix of authenticity. With wings made of resilience and audacity, it soars above the remnants of the old, charting a new course in the open skies. The phoenix is your emblem, a symbol of rebirth and the unyielding power of courageous self-expression.

As the final act, imagine the night sky ablaze with fireworks—each burst a proclamation of your individuality. The dazzling colors declare your independence from conformity, while the echoes remind you of the courage it took to stand apart. When the last firework fades, you are left with a quiet but radiant glow: the light of a life lived authentically.

Courageous self-expression is not a fleeting act; it is a daily commitment to living as your truest self. It requires dismantling the structures that stifle, rejecting the scripts that diminish, and creating a life that is uniquely, beautifully your own. The journey is not without challenges, but every step forward is a step toward liberation.

Wave your banner. Plant your garden. Paint your masterpiece. In the courageous act of self-expression, you will find the freedom to be fully, unapologetically alive.

Key Takeaways
- **Authenticity is Bold:** Break free from societal expectations and create a life that reflects your true self.
- **Destroy Conformity:** Embrace the unique and imperfect parts of yourself; they're what make you extraordinary.
- **Celebrate Your Individuality:** Like a handcrafted masterpiece, let your life reflect your quirks, passions, and truths.

- **Rewrite the Rules:** You don't need to follow anyone's blueprint. Design your path with creativity and courage.
- **Authenticity Inspires:** Living truthfully encourages others to do the same, creating a ripple effect of authenticity.

The Wild, Unrestrained Extravaganza of Life

On life's dance floor, we are all invited to the party. This isn't a careful waltz or a formal tea dance; it's a wild, unrestrained extravaganza where generosity leads and authenticity follows. So lace up your cosmic dance shoes—we're stepping into the rhythm of life's most meaningful moves.

Imagine life as a vibrant, intergalactic dance floor, pulsing with the beats of opportunity, challenge, and connection. This is not a space for wallflowers. It's your moment to step into the spotlight, where every deliberate move becomes a celebration of conscious generosity. The art of giving, when done with intention, transforms this chaotic dance into a harmonious masterpiece.

Picture generosity as the DJ spinning tracks on the turntables of life. It's not about haphazardly scattering goodwill like confetti; it's about curating moments that amplify the rhythm of connection. Each well-placed act of kindness, each thoughtful gesture, becomes a perfectly timed drop, energizing the cosmic dance floor and inspiring others to join in.

In the intricate tango of life, each step of generosity must be deliberate, an exchange of energy that elevates both the giver and the receiver. It's not about rushing through the moves but about flowing with grace and awareness. The magic lies in giving with purpose—an artful twirl, a confident dip, and a connection that resonates long after the music fades.

Traditional dances may rely on fixed steps, but life's dance floor thrives on unchoreographed authenticity. Throw away the rulebook. Dance to the beat of your heart, guided by the rhythm of generosity. Your authentic moves—the ones born of genuine care and individuality—become your signature style, inspiring others to move with freedom and purpose.

Many of us hesitate to step into the center of life's dance floor, afraid of missteps or judgment. But true generosity calls for boldness. Shake off self-doubt, abandon hesitation, and waltz into life's chaos with the radiant glow of compassion. It's not about being flawless; it's about being fearless, moving with the confidence that every step is an opportunity to make a difference.

Acts of selflessness are the salsa beats of life, infusing the ordinary with extraordinary passion and purpose. These aren't performative gestures but genuine contributions to the symphony of human connection. Each note of generosity reverberates, creating a melody that brings joy and meaning to every interaction.

Envision life's dance floor illuminated by a disco ball of kindness. Each sparkle is a random act of generosity, a moment of selflessness that lights up the room. Whether small or grand, these acts create a dazzling display of connection, reminding us that the simplest gestures can brighten even the darkest corners.

Generosity is not reserved for easy times. Picture the flamenco, with its fiery passion and resolute strength. Even in the face of adversity, courageous compassion stamps its rhythm onto the floor, radiating power and hope. Each deliberate act of care becomes a declaration: challenges may test us, but generosity keeps us moving forward.

True generosity doesn't mean overextending. It's like the controlled leaps of a ballet, where every movement is both graceful and intentional. By setting benevolent boundaries, you ensure that your giving aligns with your values and capacity. This harmony between self-care and compassion allows you to give freely without losing your footing.

Generosity is infectious. Imagine the jitterbug, its joyful swings and energetic twists sparking a chain reaction on the dance floor. When you give with joy—whether it's time, resources, or love— you invite others to join in, creating a collective rhythm of positivity that reverberates far and wide.

Empathy is the dance that connects us all, a glide into someone else's experience. It's about feeling their rhythm, understanding their tempo, and moving alongside them with compassion. This shared movement is the heartbeat of human connection, reminding us that generosity often starts with simply being present.

Generosity, like the perfect waltz, is about timing and precision. It's not about constantly giving to the point of exhaustion; it's about knowing when to step forward, when to pause, and when to pivot. Each act of care aligns with life's music, creating moments of profound impact that ripple outward.

As the music fades, what remains is the legacy of your generosity—the imprints left on the lives you've touched. Picture the night sky ablaze with fireworks, each burst a declaration of meaningful acts given freely and intentionally. This cosmic display celebrates not just what you've done but who you've become through the act of giving.

The dance floor of life is open, and the music is playing. Step boldly into the rhythm of conscious generosity, knowing that every move matters. From the simplest acts of kindness to the grandest gestures of compassion, each step contributes to the wild, unrestrained extravaganza of life.

This is your dance. Make it count.

Key Takeaways
- **Generosity as a Guide:** Purposeful generosity builds meaningful connections and amplifies your impact on the world.
- **Intentional Living:** Decide where to invest your energy, choosing actions that resonate with your values.
- **Spontaneity is Enriching:** Let moments of joy and unexpected giving add vibrancy to your life's dance.
- **Balance Giving and Receiving:** Generosity thrives when paired with boundaries that honor your well-being.
- **Small Acts, Big Impact:** Even seemingly minor gestures of kindness can create lasting ripples of positivity.

Not Your Grandma's Library

Welcome, knowledge seekers and lifelong learners, to the exhilarating pursuit of continuous learning. This is not a leisurely stroll through dusty bookshelves; it's a dynamic adventure, a journey that transforms your mind into a masterpiece. So, grab your sculptor's chisel—it's time to carve away ignorance and uncover the brilliance of intellectual growth.

The myth of the know-it-all is a trap that leads to intellectual stagnation. Believing you've reached the pinnacle of understanding is akin to abandoning a half-formed sculpture. True mastery lies not in what you already know but in the relentless pursuit of what you've yet to discover. The sculptor's chisel is ever-sharp, ready to refine, reshape, and reveal new facets of your mind.

Your mind is an evolving sculpture, a work in progress shaped by curiosity and discipline. The sculptor's chisel—symbolizing your commitment to learning—is the tool that refines rough edges and unveils hidden potential. Each stroke of the chisel represents a new insight, a deeper understanding, or an outdated belief replaced with fresh perspective. Embrace the process, for every mark made is a testament to growth.

Continuous learning requires humility. Be the stonecutter who works steadily and patiently, not the arrogant sculptor who assumes perfection. Approach the vast quarry of knowledge with respect and wonder, ready to chip away at the excess while marveling at the beauty emerging from beneath. The chisel isn't a weapon; it's an ally in the pursuit of wisdom.

Forget the image of a quiet, static library. Your intellectual sanctuary is a hub of rebellion, curiosity, and transformation. It's a place where ideas clash and evolve, where the sculptor's chisel waits for you to pick it up and shape your understanding. Make your library—whether physical or metaphorical—a fortress of intellectual adventure, stocked with the tools you need to challenge and expand your mind.

The path of continuous learning is rarely smooth. Challenges, doubts, and failures are the resistance that sharpens your chisel. Each obstacle you overcome refines your skill and strengthens your resolve. Welcome the tension—it's a necessary part of growth, forging resilience as you carve out new dimensions of understanding.

Continuous learning isn't just about acquiring knowledge; it's also about unlearning what no longer serves you. The sculptor's chisel chips away at outdated beliefs, creating space for fresh perspectives. To grow, you must let go. Approach your intellectual pursuits with openness, ready to discard the obsolete in favor of the new.

Imagine the continuous learner as a maestro conducting an orchestra of curiosity. The sculptor's chisel becomes the baton, guiding each section—science, art, philosophy—into harmony. Let the symphony of discovery play on, each note an exploration of a new idea, each movement a deeper dive into the richness of human knowledge.

Expertise is not built on a single foundation but is a mosaic of interconnected shards of knowledge. The sculptor's chisel crafts this masterpiece, shaping diverse pieces into a coherent whole. Embrace variety in your intellectual pursuits, weaving together different disciplines to create a mind that is versatile, adaptive, and rich with insights.

Be the Atlas of learning, carrying the weight of knowledge on your shoulders while exploring uncharted intellectual territories. The sculptor's chisel is your map, guiding you through the vast and often overwhelming landscape of information. Each new discovery is a step forward, and each step adds to the evolving masterpiece of your understanding.

Continuous learning is not a sprint but a marathon. Even the most dedicated sculptor knows when to pause, allowing the mind to absorb and integrate lessons learned. Moments of reflection sharpen your chisel, making it more effective for the next round of exploration. Balance effort with rest to sustain your passion for learning.

Your intellectual journey leaves behind a legacy shaped by the sculptor's chisel. Each mark—every book read, every question asked, every perspective embraced—is a testament to your dedication. Over time, your sculpture becomes a reflection of insatiable curiosity and relentless growth, inspiring others to pick up their own chisels and begin their journey.

Continuous learning is a dynamic, lifelong adventure. It requires humility, adaptability, and an unyielding commitment to growth. The sculptor's chisel, ever in motion, shapes not only what you know but also who you are. As you refine your masterpiece, remember: the journey is as important as the destination.

May your mind remain ever-malleable, your curiosity unquenchable, and your chisel ever-sharp. Go forth, lifelong learner, and carve a legacy of wisdom, growth, and boundless possibility.

Key Takeaways
- **Lifelong Learning Matters:** Keep your mind sharp and open, always ready to embrace new ideas and perspectives.
- **Unlearn to Grow:** Let go of outdated beliefs to make space for fresh insights and adaptability.
- **Curiosity Fuels Growth:** Approach learning as a fearless craftsman, eager to explore and refine your skills.
- **Diversity is Key:** Seek knowledge from different fields and viewpoints to create a richer intellectual tapestry.
- **Learning is Active:** Be an active participant in your growth by engaging, questioning, and applying what you learn.

The Oracle Within

Prepare to plunge into the mystical depths of intuition, the quiet yet powerful compass that guides us through life's uncharted waters. This isn't about mysticism in the traditional sense; it's about uncovering the wisdom that resides within, your very own oracle whispering the truths of self-awareness.

Intuition isn't brewed with eye of newt or dragon scales but distilled in the cauldron of self-awareness. It's a subtle elixir that reveals the undercurrents of your consciousness, the hidden truths that shape your decisions and guide your path. Drink deeply from this well, for its wisdom nourishes the soul.

Have you ever felt the gentle nudge of intuition, like a whisper carried on the wind? This isn't an ethereal force; it's the universe sharing its secrets, encoded in the language of your own experiences and desires. Lean in, listen closely, and let these whispers carry you toward clarity and confidence.

Think of intuition as a pirate's parley—a clandestine meeting between your conscious thoughts and the depths of your subconscious. It's not about negotiation; it's about understanding. Trust the wisdom of your inner captain, who navigates not by traditional maps but by the stars of your innermost truths.

Sailors of old had an uncanny sense for detecting storms before they appeared on the horizon. Intuition is your seafarer's sixth sense, not predicting weather but navigating life's tempests. It offers quiet warnings and gentle urgings, helping you steer clear of dangers unseen and chart a course toward calmer waters.

Picture your life as a symphony. Intuition is the conductor, not rigidly bound by the sheet music but leading with a flair for improvisation. Each movement of your life resonates with harmony when guided by the rhythm of your inner wisdom. Trust the melody unique to your journey.

In the vast darkness of uncertainty, intuition shines as a flickering lighthouse. It doesn't promise a straight line to safety but provides just enough light to guide your way. Sail confidently into the unknown, trusting that your inner beacon will illuminate the next step when it matters most.

Intuition often speaks in riddles, not to confuse you but because the language of the soul is layered and nuanced. Patience is your key to unlocking these mysteries. As you unravel its riddles, you gain profound insights into yourself, charting a path through the enigmatic depths of your being.

Think of intuition as a dowsing rod, not leading you to hidden water but to the wellspring of your true self. Each subtle movement guides you closer to authenticity. Trust its direction, for within authenticity lies the strength to face life with courage and clarity.

Gaze into the mirror of intuition—not to foresee the future, but to reflect on the present. It reveals your deepest desires, fears, and truths. The clarity it provides is a vital step toward self-mastery. Look boldly into its depths, for the reflections it offers are the keys to your growth.

Sometimes intuition wears the mask of an inner jester, playfully nudging you toward joy and spontaneity. It's not mocking you; it's reminding you to embrace life's lighter moments. Dance with the jester, let laughter fill your sails, and rediscover the joy that fuels your journey.

Intuition isn't some detached oracle; it's deeply rooted in your experiences. Its whispers are the echoes of lessons learned and insights gained. By tuning into these echoes, you transform your past into a map for navigating the present and future.

Gut feelings are the alchemical expression of intuition—transforming subtle observations into instinctive knowledge. These aren't random twinges but the distilled wisdom of your subconscious. Trust them, for they often reveal truths your conscious mind has yet to grasp.

Just as sailors relied on the stars to guide them, intuition is your internal constellation. It maps the terrain of your desires, fears, and aspirations. By trusting its light, you can chart a course through life's vast, unpredictable seas with confidence.

Opportunities carry a scent discernible only to intuition. It's not a literal fragrance but a subtle signal of potential. Inhale deeply, trust your inner sense, and let it guide you toward new shores brimming with possibilities.

For the trailblazers and rule-breakers, intuition is the compass that leads off the beaten path. It doesn't point to where others have gone; it points to where you're meant to go. Embrace its guidance, for the detours it offers often lead to the most enlightening destinations.

Creativity lives in the whispers of intuition, a muse that gently stirs your imagination. It's not a fleeting voice; it's a constant companion, urging you to create, express, and innovate. Listen closely, and let it guide your artistic pursuits to new heights.

In the symphony of life, intuition thrives in the spaces between the notes. These pauses are not voids to be filled but moments pregnant with meaning. Embrace the silence, for within it lies the profound truths your intuition is waiting to reveal.

Navigators of old followed unwritten codes; so too does intuition have its own. These aren't rules inscribed in stone but whispers etched into the fabric of your soul. By following its guidance, you'll uncover the uncharted territories of self-awareness, authenticity, and fulfillment.

Picture yourself as the captain of your own vessel, standing tall at the helm. Intuition is your compass, pointing you toward the horizon of self-discovery. Sail boldly, guided by its quiet wisdom, through the seas of uncertainty and possibility. The journey may be mysterious, but with intuition as your guide, it will also be profoundly rewarding.

Key Takeaways
- **Listen to Your Inner Compass:** Intuition is your quiet guide, helping you navigate uncertainty and complexity.

- **Balance Instinct and Logic:** Combine intuitive insights with rational thought to make confident decisions.
- **Embrace Vulnerability:** Intuition often speaks through feelings; honor them as valuable signals, not weaknesses.
- **Reflection Reveals Clarity:** Introspection strengthens your connection to your intuition and enhances self-awareness.
- **Trust the Unknown:** Intuition thrives when you allow yourself to step into the mysterious and uncharted.

Week 5

Week 5 Action Plan: Deepening Resonance and Strengthening Your Compass

As we step into Week 5, it's time to deepen the resonance of your life's symphony and strengthen the compass that guides you through chaos and harmony alike. This week focuses on inner wisdom, intentionality, and the power of authenticity in navigating life's unpredictable seas.

Day 1: "The Red Button Syndrome"
- **Activity:** Craft your own Reset Button ritual. This could be writing down habits, thoughts, or patterns you wish to release on a piece of paper and tearing it up, symbolizing your commitment to transformation. Alternatively, create a visual representation of your reset—a button you can "press" (draw or craft one) whenever you need a symbolic restart.
- **Reflection:** Reflect on what the reset symbolizes for you. How does the act of consciously choosing to reset empower you to shed outdated aspects of yourself? Consider the potential transformations this reset can initiate. How do you feel about the changes you are inviting into your life, and what steps will you take to embody this new beginning?

Day 2: "The Unsung Hero of Life"

- **Activity:** Do something that embodies your unsung qualities, something that truly reflects the essence of who you are, without seeking recognition or validation.
- **Reflection:** How does embracing and acting on your unsung qualities affect your sense of self and fulfillment?

Day 3: "The Symphony of Serendipity"

- **Activity:** Before starting your day, get a small notebook or use a digital app dedicated to note taking. Your task is to jot down any unexpected moments, chance encounters, or seemingly random occurrences that happen throughout your day. These could range from finding a book you've long wanted at a garage sale, to a chance meeting with an old friend, or even a new opportunity that comes out of a misdialed phone number.
- **Reflection:** Reflect on how these moments made you feel, any new opportunities that arose from them, and how they might be guiding you towards paths you hadn't considered. Consider continuing your Serendipity Tracking for the next week and then deeply reflecting on the role of serendipity in your life. This deeper activity and reflection are designed to tune your senses to the Symphony of Serendipity playing around you constantly. By actively engaging with serendipity, you learn to embrace the unexpected, interpreting life's subtle cues and understanding the interconnectedness of seemingly random events. This is not just about acknowledging serendipity; it's about actively inviting it into your life, allowing it to guide you to a richer, more resonant existence.

Day 4: "The Intent Matters"

- **Activity:** Before starting your day, set a clear intention for how you want to approach the day's tasks and interactions. Revisit this intention throughout the day.

- **Reflection:** Reflect on how setting an intention influenced your day. Did it change how you approached challenges or interactions?

Day 5: "It's Not About Likes and Emojis"
- **Activity:** For one day, commit to a digital detox where you consciously avoid non-essential digital distractions. This includes social media, unnecessary internet browsing, and excessive smartphone use. Focus on real-world interactions, presence, and observe the quality of these engagements.
- **Reflection:** How does the absence of digital validation impact your mood, self-esteem, and connections with others? Did the absence of these distractions illuminate any habitual patterns or dependencies on technology? How can you integrate the insights gained from this experience to better steer through life's digital sea without losing sight of your true course?

Day 6: "Storms Don't Weaken Your Lighthouse"
- **Activity:** Write a letter to yourself about a past challenge you've overcome. Highlight the strengths you displayed and how you can apply them to current or future challenges.
- **Reflection:** In what ways are you your own lighthouse, guiding yourself through life's storms with resilience and strength? What core values make up the light of your lighthouse, and how do they guide you in difficult times? How can you maintain and strengthen your light to ensure it continues to guide you and others?

Day 7: Weekly Integration - Mastering Intentions
- **Activity:** Create a personal intention-setting ritual. Begin by writing down your core values and the intentions you wish to manifest in your life. Place these written intentions somewhere you will see them daily. For one week, start each day by reading your intentions aloud and visualize yourself living these intentions fully.

- **Reflection:** After completing your intention-setting ritual, reflect on how aligning your daily actions with your intentions changes your perspective and actions. Consider the following questions: How does setting clear intentions influence your decisions? How do you feel when your actions are in harmony with your intentions?

This week aims to reinforce your inner strength, clarity, and resilience. By focusing on your oracle within, acknowledging your triggers, setting intentions, honoring your unsung hero, disconnecting from superficial validation, and reaffirming your resilience, you fortify your ability to navigate life's symphony with purpose and impact. Carry these lessons forward as you continue to orchestrate a life of meaningful resonance and authentic balance.

The Red Button Syndrome

You've seen the red button in cartoons—the one you're warned never to press. Forget that. Smash it. The Reset Button isn't about a delicate tap; it's about full-blown transformation. Pressing reset is not a small adjustment; it's an act of reinvention, a bold leap into the unknown.

Imagine standing on the edge of a cliff, staring into the vast unknown. The Reset Button isn't an anchor; it's your parachute. It's a leap of liberation—a fearless dive into the exhilarating chaos of change. By pressing it, you shed old skins, outdated patterns, and limiting expectations, emerging as something entirely new.

Over time, we collect identities like dusty books on a forgotten shelf—old labels, worn-out roles, and narratives that no longer serve us. The Reset Button clears the clutter. It's a detox for the soul, a purge of all that's outdated and unnecessary. With one bold push, you create space for authenticity and possibility.

Resetting your life is not a slow, incremental shift; it's a quantum leap. It's about rejecting limitations and stepping into a reality where the impossible becomes possible. The Reset Button doesn't wait for probabilities—it transforms them into certainties, opening doors you didn't even know existed.

Life is a symphony, but who says you have to play by the conventional notes? The Reset Button is your conductor's baton, empowering you to rewrite the music. Toss out the sheet music of expectations and compose a melody that reflects your individuality, a symphony of subversion against the mundane.

Ever feel like a puppet tangled in society's expectations? The Reset Button is your pair of scissors, slicing through the cords that hold you back. It's your declaration of independence, freeing you to move according to your own will and desires.

The concept of tabula rasa—a blank slate—isn't just philosophical; it's a call to action. The Reset Button wipes away old narratives, giving you the freedom to create something entirely new. With it, life becomes a canvas, and you hold the brush. What will you paint?

Time travelers wrestle with the question of where to go next: the past, the future, or somewhere entirely different. The Reset Button offers a different perspective—it grounds you in the present. It's not about reliving what was or worrying about what could be; it's about embracing the now with clarity and intention.

Resetting isn't calm or gentle—it's a storm. The Reset Button stirs the winds of transformation, scattering the old and making way for the new. Chaos isn't something to fear; it's the birthplace of clarity. Within the storm lies the power to redefine yourself.

Life often comes with permission slips handed out by society—rules for how to behave, what to pursue, and who to be. The

Reset Button shreds those permissions and declares your autonomy. You don't need approval to change your life; you only need the courage to press reset.

Life can feel heavy at times, like carrying the weight of lead. But the Reset Button is your alchemist's tool, transforming that heaviness into the gold of new opportunities and aspirations. It's not magic; it's the power of reinvention.

Much like a phoenix rising from the ashes, the Reset Button ignites transformation. It doesn't dwell on the remnants of the past; it embraces the flames of renewal. Through this act, you rise stronger, brighter, and more aligned with your true self.

Life isn't a binary system of yes or no, success or failure. The Reset Button dismantles those rigid codes and opens the door to infinite possibilities. It allows you to write your own script, one that reflects your dreams and aspirations, rather than society's expectations.

In a world full of noise, resetting creates a moment of silence—a pause to reconnect with your inner melody. The Reset Button is your tuning fork, harmonizing your life with the resonance of authenticity. In the quiet, you'll find your truest rhythm.

Gravity may hold the ordinary in place, but the Reset Button is for those ready to defy it. It's your wings, propelling you to heights you never thought possible. By pressing it, you soar beyond the constraints of the familiar into the boundless skies of potential.

Echo chambers confine us, repeating the same thoughts, ideas, and patterns. The Reset Button is your sledgehammer, breaking down those walls and allowing fresh ideas and perspectives to flood in. It's not just about resetting; it's about breaking free.

Smashing the Reset Button isn't a mere action—it's a commitment to transformation. It's about reclaiming control, rewriting your narrative, and embracing the unknown with courage and excitement. Are you ready to press it? The journey awaits. It starts with a single, bold step into a future of your own design.

Key Takeaways

- **Change is Power:** Reinvention isn't a failure; it's a bold act of growth and transformation.
- **Release the Old:** Let go of outdated identities and beliefs that no longer serve your journey.
- **Embrace Uncertainty:** The unknown holds the potential for reinvention; approach it with curiosity and courage.
- **Resets are Essential:** Periodically evaluate your life's trajectory and don't fear starting over if needed.
- **Reinvention Builds Resilience:** Each reset strengthens your ability to adapt and thrive in the face of change.

The Unsung Hero of Life

In the exhilarating realm of open-mindedness lies the unsung hero of human growth: discernment. It's the quiet force that guides us through the symphony of life, helping us sift through the cacophony of ideas to find meaning and understanding. Buckle up, because we're diving deep into the art of discernment—a skill that blends curiosity, critical thinking, and emotional intelligence into a masterful practice of open exploration.

Discernment is no passive act. It's a mental gymnastics routine—a dynamic choreography of curiosity and critical thinking that flips, twists, and balances through the landscape of ideas. It's about embracing the panoramic view of possibility and moving with intention through the intellectual terrain, uncovering treasures along the way.

Imagine yourself as an intrepid explorer of the intellectual realm, navigating with an open mind instead of a compass. The journey of discernment takes you through the dense jungles of perspectives, up the peaks of ideologies, and into the valleys of conflicting opinions. It's not about avoiding uncertainty but diving into it, embracing complexity as an invitation to grow.

Discernment begins by letting go of the illusion of certainty. Growth happens in the shades of gray, where ambiguity thrives, and questions often lead to more questions. Embrace this uncertainty as fertile ground for intellectual expansion—a space where possibilities flourish, and growth becomes inevitable.

Mastering discernment requires unlearning old habits, biases, and assumptions. It's like peeling away the layers of an onion—shedding societal conditioning and self-imposed limitations to reveal a clearer, more nuanced understanding. With each layer removed, you draw closer to the core of truth and self-awareness.

Consider your discernment as a wardrobe filled with eclectic garments, each representing a different perspective. You have the liberty to mix and match, trying on new viewpoints to see how they fit. This sartorial celebration of intellectual diversity reminds us that no single outfit—or idea—defines us.

Discernment equips you with a mental toolbox. Inside, you'll find the screwdriver of skepticism, the wrench of empathy, and the pliers of critical thinking. The skilled craftsman knows which tool to use for each task, shaping a nuanced understanding of the world with precision and care.

Balancing openness with critical evaluation is like walking a tightrope. Discernment requires grace and finesse, a steady ability to weigh ideas without falling into the chasm of dogma or blind acceptance. Imagine yourself as a tightrope walker, maintaining equilibrium as you navigate the ever-shifting landscape of thoughts.

Discernment isn't all seriousness; it's also a playground of curiosity. Each idea is a swing, inviting you to take it for a spin. By embracing the playfulness of intellectual exploration, you can swing between perspectives, perform somersaults of thought, and discover unexpected insights with joy and freedom.

At its core, discernment demands humility. It's the recognition that your understanding is just a small corner of the vast expanse of human thought. Each perspective you encounter adds to the collective wisdom, reminding you that we all contribute to the shared laughter and discovery of life's playground.

Picture discernment as hosting a dinner party for ideas. Each thought arrives as a guest, bringing its unique flavor to the table. Your role as host is to orchestrate this intellectual feast, savoring the diversity of viewpoints while ensuring each one has its moment to shine.

Discernment is not only about logic; it's about understanding the emotions that underpin ideas. Emotional intelligence becomes the secret sauce, allowing you to empathize with the feelings behind each perspective. By engaging with both the rational and the emotional, you build a deeper, more holistic understanding.

Your mind is like a yoga mat for discernment. Stretch your mental flexibility by assuming the poses of various viewpoints, finding balance between strength and suppleness. Just as physical yoga builds resilience, this intellectual practice strengthens your ability to adapt and grow.

In the intellectual cosmos, discernment connects the dots to form constellations of understanding. It's the ability to see relationships between ideas, recognize patterns, and discover new stars in the galaxy of knowledge. Each connection expands your awareness, adding depth and meaning to your perspective.

A discerning mind is also a reflective one. It's a mirror that not only examines external ideas but also scrutinizes internal biases and assumptions. Regular self-reflection clears the fog, offering clarity and ensuring that your discernment remains sharp and unbiased.

Discernment takes courage. It's about venturing into unknown intellectual territories, confronting the dragons of ignorance, and challenging your own cognitive comfort zones. This bravery propels you toward deeper truths and a richer understanding of the world.

Discernment is not a destination but an ever-expanding journey. It's a labyrinth of ideas where each turn reveals a new facet of understanding. Envision your mind as an infinity mirror, reflecting and refracting thoughts in endless exploration.

As you navigate the rich terrain of open-mindedness, remember: discernment is more than a skill—it's the compass that guides you through the labyrinth of ideas. Keep your mind open, your tools ready, and your curiosity alive. The intellectual playground awaits, and you are its fearless maestro, orchestrating the symphony of diverse thoughts.

Key Takeaways
- **Balance Openness and Skepticism:** Explore new ideas while critically evaluating their value to your life.
- **Unlearning is Growth:** Releasing outdated assumptions creates space for nuanced understanding.
- **Humility Fuels Wisdom:** Recognize the limits of your knowledge and remain curious about other perspectives.

- **Diversity Enriches Thinking:** Engage with viewpoints different from your own to expand your intellectual horizons.
- **Practice Discernment:** Thoughtfully weigh decisions and ideas instead of reacting impulsively.

The Intent Matters

A treasure map lies before you, but instead of "X marks the spot," the map reads, "P marks your purpose." Dust off your explorer's hat, grab your compass, and prepare to embark on an exhilarating journey to uncover the hidden treasures of a life lived with intent.

Every purposeful journey begins with a compass—a steadfast commitment to intentional living. Life isn't about wandering aimlessly through the forest of existence; it's about forging your own path. With the machete of purpose in hand, you carve a trail that aligns with your values, vision, and passions.

Life presents a series of crossroads, and purpose is your GPS. Purposeful living doesn't mean blindly following a predefined route. It's about rejecting autopilot navigation, taking the scenic path, and fully engaging with the journey. With purpose as your guide, every choice becomes an opportunity for meaningful direction.

As you traverse the landscapes of purpose, your backpack is packed with your values—the non-negotiable essentials that sustain you on the journey. These aren't trinkets picked up from the souvenir shop of societal expectations; they're deeply personal principles that give your path its unique shape.

In the desert of the mundane, purpose reveals an oasis of passion. This isn't a fleeting mirage; it's a source of vitality and joy. Dive into this wellspring, let it invigorate you, and allow it to fuel a life that feels richly and authentically lived.

Hidden along the path of purposeful living lies the treasure chest of your talents. Purpose acts as the map that leads you to these hidden abilities—skills and strengths you didn't know you possessed. By unlocking this chest, you unleash the tools needed to thrive and contribute meaningfully to the world.

Purposeful living involves scaling the mountains of challenges. These climbs aren't meant to be avoided; they're meant to be conquered. The ascent builds resilience, and when you plant your flag at the summit, you'll understand the strength that comes from persevering through the climb.

Along the journey, the quicksands of distraction threaten to pull you off course. Purpose acts as your map, helping you identify these treacherous terrains and navigate around them. Staying focused on your purpose ensures you don't sink into the traps of mindless pursuits.

In purposeful living, you'll find the river of flow—a state of harmony where effort feels effortless. It's not about fighting the current but navigating it with a kayak named Purpose. As you follow its twists and turns, you'll discover the beauty of being fully immersed in your journey.

Amid the purposeful jungle stands the Forest of Reflection. Each tree bears the marks of your personal growth, its rings telling the story of your evolving purpose. Purposeful living invites you to pause, sit on the mossy ground, and contemplate how far you've come.

Every step you take sends ripples through the world. Purposeful living turns those ripples into resounding echoes of impact. It's not about tiptoeing through life but stepping boldly, creating meaningful change, and letting your purposeful actions reverberate far and wide.

Purposeful living doesn't avoid the canyons of difficulty—it builds bridges across them. These challenges aren't obstacles; they're opportunities to strengthen your resolve. With purpose as your foundation, resilience becomes your wings, lifting you over life's deepest chasms.

As you sail the seas of purposeful living, let your values guide you like the North Star. Purposeful living isn't reckless or aimless; it's deliberate and principled, driven by the constellations of what matters most to you.

In the fertile soil of purposeful living grows the Garden of Relationships. These connections are nurtured by mutual respect, shared goals, and moments of joy. Purposeful living prioritizes cultivating relationships that bloom with meaning and enrich your journey.

Perched high on the cliffs of purposeful living stands the Lighthouse of Legacy, casting its light across the waves of time.

Living with purpose isn't about leaving behind fleeting marks; it's about building a legacy that continues to guide others long after your journey has carried you to new horizons.

Purposeful living anchors in the Archipelago of Curiosity, where exploration fuels growth. It's not about staying docked in one port but sailing from island to island, driven by an insatiable desire to learn, grow, and expand your understanding of the world.

Gaze through the Telescope of Vision, and purposeful living reveals constellations invisible to the naked eye. It's not about short-term gains but seeing the big picture—a future shaped by your actions, dreams, and deeply held intentions.

At the summit of purposeful living lies the Observatory of Introspection. This isn't a race to the top; it's a place to pause, reflect, and marvel at the vastness of your purpose. From this vantage point, you see the interconnectedness of your journey and the beauty of your unfolding story.

When you live with purpose, your life becomes a Symphony of Alignment. Each note resonates with meaning, each movement builds harmony, and every instrument plays in sync with your deepest intentions. This is the melody of a life well-lived—a masterpiece shaped by purpose.

The compass of intention and the map of purpose lead not to a far-off destination but to a place called Home. Home is where your heart beats in alignment with your purpose, where your life feels true to who you are and what you value most.

So, fellow explorer, set your compass, unfold your map, and venture forth into the vast landscapes of purposeful living. The treasure of a life lived with intent awaits, ready to be claimed by those brave enough to chart their own course.

Key Takeaways

- **Purpose as a Guide:** A clear sense of purpose provides direction and helps prioritize what matters most.
- **Align Actions with Values:** Purposeful living means making choices that resonate with your core beliefs.
- **Set Meaningful Goals:** Define objectives that inspire and motivate you to keep moving forward.
- **Reject Drift:** Avoid aimlessness by consistently realigning with your purpose.
- **Small Steps Add Up:** Purposeful living isn't about grand gestures but about small, consistent actions that build momentum.

The Symphony of Serendipity

In life's vast, intricate web, each strand a potential pathway, each intersection a crossroads of choices and chances. Within this web, the Symphony of Serendipity plays its enchanting tune, inviting us to step into the flow of the unforeseen, to dance with the unknown. Serendipity is more than coincidence; it's the universe's playful whisper—a nudge toward opportunities cloaked in randomness. It's the cosmos saying, "Trust me," with a mischievous wink, beckoning you to join a game whose rules are unwritten but whose rewards are limitless.

To the untrained ear, the Symphony of Serendipity may sound like chaos. But to those who truly listen, it reveals itself as a masterpiece of interconnected melodies. Each note represents a chance encounter or an unexpected opportunity; each pause is a moment of reflection, and each crescendo propels you toward a purpose you may not yet fully understand. This is the music of life's unscripted moments, where spontaneity becomes the stage, and we—the actors—navigate the improvisational choreography of existence.

Serendipity is not passive. It's not about sitting back and waiting for fate to intervene. Instead, it demands an active participant—someone attuned to life's subtle cues, ready to pivot with grace and leap with courage when the moment arises. Think of serendipity as life's improvisation: no rehearsals, no second takes. It's about embracing each moment, making choices in real time, and trusting that these decisions will lead you exactly where you're meant to go, even if it's far from where you initially planned.

The Symphony of Serendipity thrives on openness. Open your mind, your heart, and your eyes to the wonder that surrounds you. Life-changing opportunities often come disguised as mundane moments or unexpected challenges. Serendipity rewards the bold—those who dare to dream, step outside their comfort zones, and embrace the possibilities hidden in the unknown.

Your serendipitous experiences are uniquely yours—a melody that weaves through the symphony of your life. What feels like a misstep to one person may be the pivotal note in another's crescendo. Yet serendipity is also a shared experience. Our individual melodies intertwine, creating complex harmonies. A chance encounter in your life can ripple outward, altering the course of others in profound and unexpected ways.

To dance to the Symphony of Serendipity is to find joy in the journey, not just the destination. It's about celebrating the here and now, appreciating the beauty of fleeting moments, and recognizing each one as a stepping stone toward your ultimate purpose. This is where the magic of serendipity shines—when we learn to trust the process and savor the spontaneity of life.

Navigating the Symphony of Serendipity requires mindfulness, like a conductor guiding an orchestra. It's about being present, attuned to the rhythms of life, and ready to adapt as the music shifts. Resilience is also essential, as not every opportunity will lead where you hope. Some paths may end in dissonance, but every experience—pleasant or not—adds depth to the composition. Learn from the discord, adjust your tempo, and keep playing.

Trust is the foundation of serendipity. Trust in the journey, in the chaos, and in yourself. Believe that you are where you need to be, even if the path seems uncertain. Life often works in ways we can't predict, but faith in the process allows serendipity to flourish, transforming chance into purpose.

The Symphony of Serendipity isn't about finding a straight path to happiness or success. It's about embracing the beauty of life's detours, learning from setbacks, and discovering joy in surprises. Like an unexpected twist in a melody, these moments add richness and texture to the larger composition.

Patience is essential in the symphony. The most magical moments often unfold when least expected. Like seeds breaking through soil, serendipity requires time to bloom. Courage, too, plays a crucial role. It takes bravery to follow an uncharted path, say yes to the unknown, and leap into uncertainty with faith that you'll land exactly where you need to be.

Reflection is the quiet melody playing in the background of serendipity. In stillness, you can hear life's whispers, guiding you toward your next adventure. It's through introspection that you connect the dots, find meaning in the seemingly random, and prepare for what lies ahead.

Embracing serendipity requires a spirit of adventure. Life isn't a problem to solve but a mystery to explore. The Symphony of Serendipity invites you to uncover hidden treasures, discover unexpected connections, and revel in the wonder of it all. This is not a passive journey; it's an active pursuit of the unknown with curiosity as your compass.

As the grand theater of life continues, so does the Symphony of Serendipity. The music evolves, shifting with the rhythm of your choices and the tempo of your trust. In this symphony, there are no accidents—only serendipitous moments waiting to be embraced.

Take a bow, dear conductor. The symphony is yours to guide, the melodies yours to create. With an open heart, a curious mind, and a courageous spirit, let the Symphony of Serendipity be the soundtrack to a life lived fully, fearlessly, and with infinite possibility.

Key Takeaways
- **Be Open to Possibilities:** Life's detours often lead to surprising and meaningful outcomes.
- **Trust the Process:** Even moments of chaos can contribute to the bigger picture of your journey.
- **Seize Serendipitous Moments:** Act when chance aligns with opportunity, and make the most of unexpected openings.
- **Curiosity Unlocks Doors:** Stay curious and receptive to the world's hidden connections and patterns.

- **Find Beauty in Detours:** Serendipity often resides in the unplanned; embrace life's twists and turns with optimism.

It's Not About Likes and Emojis

Grab your compass, because we're navigating the labyrinth of relationships with the boldness of explorers and the wisdom of sages. This isn't a guide to superficial bonds or fleeting encounters—it's a manifesto for forging connections that resonate, endure, and define the rich tapestry of our lives.

Imagine a world where relationships are measured in likes and emojis, where connections are curated and filtered through the lens of social media. Superficiality thrives here, reducing human interaction to a parade of highlights. But we're not here to compete in virtual popularity contests. Real connections are messy, tangible, and beautifully imperfect, forged in the rawness of shared experiences.

In a world where swipes dictate romantic possibilities, it's easy to get caught in the Tinder tango of superficial attraction. But this isn't about collecting matches like trophies. Real connection requires stepping beyond pixelated profiles and curated bios, finding resonance in the quirks, complexities, and laughter of genuine human interaction.

Superficiality reduces emotions to emojis—a heart-eyed face for love, a crying face for pain. But relationships can't be encapsulated in cartoon icons. They thrive on full sentences, messy emotions, and conversations where vulnerability outweighs perfection. Authentic connections demand the rich language of honesty and openness, far beyond what an emoji can express.

Superficiality is the masquerade where people wear carefully crafted identities, hiding their true selves behind digital personas. But we're not here for shallow connections built on illusion. Real relationships thrive in the vulnerability of unmasking—showing up as our true selves and accepting others for who they are, flaws and all.

In a culture obsessed with friend counts and follower numbers, superficiality equates connection with quantity. But life isn't about amassing a legion of acquaintances; it's about cultivating a tight-knit crew of genuine relationships. These are the people who see you clearly, know you deeply, and stand by you unwaveringly.

Imagine relationships as brushstrokes on the canvas of your life. Each connection adds depth and color, painting a masterpiece of shared experiences. This isn't about staging perfect selfies or curating Instagram-worthy moments; it's about creating authentic memories that remind us of our shared humanity.

Superficiality strives for airbrushed perfection, where flaws are erased and relationships are polished to a sterile shine. But real connections celebrate the "flawsome"—the beauty in imperfections, quirks, and vulnerabilities. It's in these raw, unfiltered moments that the strongest bonds are formed.

Relationships aren't accessories to be paraded on a runway of social approval. They're not about showcasing a perfect lineup of associations. Instead, they're deeply personal connections, unique and irreplaceable. Real bonds aren't built for display—they're the quiet, powerful undercurrent shaping who we are.

Superficiality traps relationships in an echo chamber of glossy narratives, amplifying the same shallow notes. But real connections disrupt this symphony with new, authentic harmonies. They introduce the melodies of diversity, depth, and genuine human experience, creating music that resonates far beyond the superficial.

Superficiality burdens relationships with impossible expectations—perfect appearances, flawless interactions, and unattainable ideals. But real connection sheds this weight, embracing the beauty of authenticity. It's about accepting relationships for what they are: imperfect, evolving, and deeply human.

Superficiality follows a script of conformity, dictating how relationships should look and feel. But we're not here to read from someone else's narrative. We're here to write our own stories—filled with unfiltered emotions, unscripted moments, and the courage to be unapologetically ourselves.

Flaws aren't imperfections to be hidden; they're the defining features of real relationships. Embracing flaws—both our own and those of others—is an act of courage. It's a declaration that authenticity matters more than perfection, that real beauty lies in the messy, wonderful chaos of being human.

In a world of digital facades and curated personas, authenticity becomes a radical act. Relationships thrive when we step out from behind the masks and let our true selves shine. Vulnerability becomes the brush, and honesty the paint, as we create masterpieces of connection on the canvas of shared experiences.

Superficial relationships follow a predictable rhythm, a loop of shallow echoes. But genuine connections introduce unexpected harmonies and complex layers. They transform the symphony of human interaction into a masterpiece of depth, resonance, and profound meaning.

In the end, relationships aren't about likes, emojis, or curated appearances. They're about showing up, being seen, and seeing others in their truest form. It's about embracing the messiness, the laughter, the tears, and the unspoken moments that make human connection so profound.

So, drop the filters, ditch the hashtags, and step boldly into the real. This isn't about building a gallery of superficial connections—it's about creating a legacy of authenticity, one genuine bond at a time.

Key Takeaways
- **Depth Over Superficiality:** Authentic connections are built on trust, vulnerability, and shared experiences, not surface-level interactions.
- **Quality Over Quantity:** Focus on meaningful relationships rather than accumulating acquaintances or followers.
- **Celebrate Imperfections:** Real connections thrive in the messiness of human complexity.
- **Authenticity is Key:** Show up as your true self and create space for others to do the same.

- **Invest in Connection:** Relationships require effort and intentionality; nurture them with care and sincerity.

Storms Don't Weaken Your Lighthouse

Life's unpredictable seas are filled with waves of challenges, undercurrents of societal pressure, and the occasional tsunami of chaos. In the midst of these tempests stands your lighthouse—your integrity—radiating a steady light to guide you through the storm. It's the unshakable beacon that ensures you remain true to your course, no matter how turbulent the waters become.

Imagine your core values as the vibrant light shining from the lighthouse of integrity. These values aren't static or dusty relics; they're dynamic and alive, piercing through the darkness to illuminate your path. When life's seas get rough, it's your values that keep you steady, a reminder of the principles you hold dear.

In the vast ocean of life, sirens call out, tempting you toward the dangerous rocks of compromise. Integrity acts as your earplugs, drowning out their seductive songs. It's the steadfast refusal to be swayed by the allure of shortcuts or expediency—a constant commitment to living authentically.

Integrity isn't a fixed destination; it's a journey of constant course correction. Think of it as a compass, always pointing you toward your true north. Regular self-reflection becomes the sailor's tool, helping you navigate away from detours and align with the authentic path shaped by your core values.

Picture the shipwrecks along the shores of convenience—remnants of vessels that chose the easy route over the right one. These wrecks are cautionary tales, reminders that integrity is the lighthouse that prevents you from straying into dangerous waters. It's your safeguard against the erosion of principles.

Every lighthouse needs a keeper, and your integrity is no exception. You are its caretaker, responsible for ensuring its flame burns bright. This means regularly polishing the lens, trimming the wick, and standing watch through the night to ensure that your values shine clearly, even in the fog of societal expectations.

Life is often shrouded in the fog of ethical dilemmas, where the right path isn't always obvious. In these moments, your lighthouse becomes a powerful guide, cutting through uncertainty with the clarity of your principles. Integrity doesn't waver, even when the fog thickens.

The seas may batter your lighthouse with waves of adversity, but it stands firm, unwavering in its purpose. Similarly, integrity isn't about never being challenged; it's about staying true despite the challenges. Storms may come, but they only strengthen your resolve to remain authentic.

Your integrity isn't a single monolith; it's a mosaic, each piece representing a unique value—honesty, compassion, resilience—working together to create the vibrant picture of your character.

It's the artful arrangement of these values that makes your integrity strong and enduring.

On the darkest nights, when the stars are hidden and the seas are rough, your integrity becomes your guiding celestial body. It's the light you navigate by, reassuring you that you're on the right course, even when the destination feels impossibly far away.

Imagine your lighthouse standing tall on a desolate shore, its light shining brightly despite the isolation. This solitude represents the strength of your integrity—the ability to remain steadfast in your values, even without external validation. True integrity doesn't depend on applause; it thrives in quiet conviction.

Life's waters are filled with shadows of temptation, enticing you to drift off course. Integrity is your anchor, holding you firm against these currents. It's the steady force that keeps you aligned with what truly matters, regardless of external pressures.

There will be moments when the flame of your lighthouse flickers—moments of moral challenge, self-doubt, or unexpected setbacks. Yet, like any dedicated keeper, you tend to the flame, nurturing it back to full strength. Integrity isn't about being flawless; it's about resilience and the courage to reignite your light.

Consider the ship of accountability arriving at your harbor. It's not a vessel of judgment but a partner in ensuring you stay true to your course. Integrity is the harbormaster, welcoming accountability as a tool for growth and self-correction.

The light of your lighthouse doesn't just guide you; it impacts the waves that crash against the shore, sending ripples outward. Your integrity inspires those around you, encouraging them to navigate their own lives with authenticity and purpose.

Storms don't weaken your lighthouse; they fortify it. Challenges aren't meant to erode your integrity but to forge it into a formidable force. Each tempest you weather becomes a testament to your unwavering commitment to live authentically, a reminder of your ability to stand firm when tested.

The light from your lighthouse moves in a rhythmic beam—a steady, reliable presence. Integrity works the same way. It's not an occasional act but a consistent melody, the heartbeat of your values played out in the choices you make each day.

Your lighthouse casts a shadow that stretches beyond your journey. This is your legacy—the enduring impact of a life lived with integrity. It's a beacon for others, a symbol of resilience, authenticity, and the power of staying true to one's values.

In the unpredictable seas of life, your lighthouse is your steadfast guide. Its light doesn't falter in the face of storms; it shines brighter, illuminating the path forward. Be the keeper of your light, tending to your integrity with care, and let it guide you and others toward safe harbors. The storms may rage, but your lighthouse will stand, a testament to the strength and beauty of living authentically.

Key Takeaways
- **Integrity is Your Beacon:** Your core values are the light guiding you through life's challenges and ethical dilemmas.
- **Stay Steadfast in Storms:** Challenges don't erode integrity—they strengthen your commitment to live authentically.
- **Regularly Reflect:** Self-reflection ensures your actions align with your principles, keeping your light steady.

- **Inspire Others:** Living with integrity leaves a legacy, encouraging others to navigate their lives with authenticity.
- **Strength in Solitude:** True integrity shines even when there's no audience, proving its worth in quiet conviction.

Week 6

Week 6 Action Plan: Navigating Uncharted Waters

Welcome to Week 6, where we dive into the final chapters of "Harmony in the Chaos" to navigate the uncharted waters of life with agility, purpose, and balance. This week, you'll harness the full power of your internal compass, embrace life's unpredictable curveballs, and chart a course toward true liberation and balance.

Day 1: "Master that Compass Already!"
- **Activity:** Design your personal compass. On a piece of paper, draw a compass and label the four directions with your core values. Place this compass somewhere you will see it daily.
- **Reflection:** How do your core values guide your daily decisions and long-term goals?

Day 2: "The Occasional Cosmic Curveball"
- **Activity:** Reflect on a recent "curveball" life threw at you. Write about how you responded, what you learned, and how you might handle similar unexpected events in the future.
- **Reflection:** What does this curveball teach you about your resilience and adaptability?

Day 3: "The Map to Liberation"
- **Activity:** Create a "Map to Liberation" by listing resentments and grudges you are carrying. Next to each, write at least one action you can take to liberate yourself.
- **Reflection:** How does envisioning your path to liberation make you feel, and which burdensome weights you most excited to rid yourself of?

Day 4: "Back to the Garden of Priorities"
- **Activity:** Spend time in nature or a place that brings you peace. Contemplate your priorities and how they've shifted throughout this journey.
- **Reflection:** In what ways has reconnecting with your priorities in a peaceful setting provided clarity or new insights?

Day 5: "Unlike Jellyfish, Take Aim"
- **Activity:** Set a specific, measurable goal related to a personal project or aspiration. Outline the steps you need to take to achieve this goal.
- **Reflection:** How does setting a clear aim empower you to move forward with intention?

Day 6: "Life's Balancing Act"
- **Activity:** For the next week, practice a physical balance exercise (e.g., yoga, standing on one foot) as a metaphor for life's balance. While you are balancing, reflect on the areas of your life that need more balance.
- **Reflection:** What did the physical act of balancing teach you about maintaining equilibrium in your life?

Day 7: Weekly Integration - Charting Your Course
- **Activity:** Combine insights from this week into a "Life's Course Chart." This could be a visual representation, written plan, or another creative format that maps out how you'll navigate life's complexities with your newly sharpened compass.

- **Reflection:** Reflect on the journey you've undertaken during these six weeks. How have your perspectives shifted, and how do you feel equipped to handle the chaos and harmony of life?

This week's journey brings you to the helm of your life's ship, with a firm grip on your compass, eyes on the horizon, and a heart ready for whatever the seas may bring. As you continue to navigate the waters of life, remember that your compass, crafted from your deepest values and lessons learned, will always guide you back to your true north. Keep charting your course with courage, curiosity, and an unwavering commitment to your journey of growth and impact.

Master that Compass Already!

We're diving into the art of mastering your internal compass—the emotional tool that guides you through life's unpredictable seas. Emotional resilience isn't just about surviving the storm; it's about learning to ride the waves like a seasoned surfer of the soul. So, buckle up, emotional adventurer, because the seas ahead are as wild as they are transformative.

Life's emotional landscape is as changeable as the open sea. One moment, the waters are calm; the next, you're caught in a tempest of anger, sadness, or anxiety. Emotional resilience isn't about avoiding these tempests but learning to navigate through them with skill and grace. Just like a seasoned sailor trusts their tools, you must trust your internal compass to find emotional balance amidst the chaos.

Your internal compass, much like a sailor's, needs regular calibration. Life has a way of throwing magnetic disturbances your way—a heartbreak, a setback, or just one of those inexplicably hard days. Emotional resilience is about recognizing these disruptions and recalibrating your compass so it always points toward your emotional true north: balance, clarity, and self-compassion.

Emotional weather is as unpredictable as a summer storm. Sunny serenity can give way to turbulent thunderstorms without warning. Emotional resilience is your inner meteorologist, helping you interpret the forecast and prepare for whatever turbulence comes your way. It's not about eliminating storms but understanding their patterns and learning how to weather them.

Surf's up! Emotional resilience means mastering the art of emotional surfing—finding balance and flow on the waves of your feelings. Whether it's the exhilarating highs of joy or the crashing lows of sorrow, the key is to ride each wave with finesse and a sense of humor. You can't control the waves, but you can choose how to ride them.

Picture the rogue waves of life crashing against your emotional vessel. These waves represent the unforeseen challenges, sudden setbacks, or unexpected twists that can leave you reeling. Emotional resilience isn't about preventing these waves from appearing—it's about becoming the captain who skillfully steers through them, staying steady amidst the chaos.

Ever seen a surfer ride a monstrous wave with calm determination? Emotional resilience is about channeling your inner stoic surfer. It's the ability to maintain your balance, composure, and focus, even when towering emotions threaten to knock you off your board. Resilience is the art of staying grounded while the seas of life churn around you.

Sometimes emotions come in tidal waves—intense, overwhelming, and seemingly unstoppable. Emotional resilience isn't about avoiding these waves but about constructing an emotional seawall. This seawall is built with self-awareness, coping strategies, and the strength to stand firm when emotions surge.

Emotional currents are fluid, shifting, and often unpredictable. They can twist and turn without warning, much like the glowing streams of a lava lamp. Emotional resilience means embracing this fluidity—acknowledging that emotions are in constant motion and learning to flow with them rather than resist.

In the vast emotional ocean, you are the captain of your ship. A compassionate captain doesn't scold themselves for feeling anger, sadness, or fear. Instead, they acknowledge their emotions, accept them without judgment, and gently steer toward calmer waters. Self-compassion is the anchor that grounds you when the seas become overwhelming.

Amidst the storms, there are hidden archipelagos of joy, laughter, and contentment. Emotional resilience isn't just about surviving the hardships—it's also about seeking and savoring these moments of light. Setting your course for these islands reminds you that even in the roughest seas, there are places of peace and happiness waiting to be discovered.

Mastering your emotional compass is a lifelong journey, but with each storm you navigate and each wave you ride, your skills will grow. Resilience isn't about never feeling lost—it's about trusting that, with your compass in hand and a steady heart, you'll always find your way back to calm waters. So, captain, set your sights on the horizon and sail boldly forward. The seas may be wild, but you are more than ready for the adventure.

Your emotional life is a symphony—a blend of serene sonatas and stormy overtures. Emotional resilience is the art of conducting this symphony, transforming the cacophony of feelings into a harmonious melody that aligns with your internal compass. It's not about silencing emotions but orchestrating them into a balanced, resonant rhythm that guides you forward.

Imagine yourself as the conductor of your emotional symphony, wielding the baton of resilience. Each feeling—joy, anger, sorrow, hope—plays its part in creating a masterpiece. Emotional resilience isn't about eliminating dissonance but about blending these emotional notes into a melody that resonates with authenticity and inner balance.

Just as the sun sets each day, emotional resilience teaches you to release feelings that no longer serve you. Every emotional sunset clears the horizon for a new dawn, paving the way for renewal and clarity. Letting go becomes an essential navigational tool, helping you chart a course toward brighter emotional landscapes.

Life's emotional map includes vast, uncharted territories—lands of fear, grief, and uncertainty. Emotional resilience transforms you into an intrepid explorer, ready to venture into these mysterious spaces. Within them, you'll uncover hidden treasures of self-awareness, growth, and untapped strength.

Alchemy isn't just the mythical transformation of lead into gold; it's also the process of turning emotional challenges into profound wisdom. Emotional resilience is your internal alchemist, helping you transform the heaviness of fear or sadness into the gold of growth, clarity, and deeper self-understanding.

In the stormy seas of emotion, your internal compass doubles as a lighthouse, casting a steady beam of guidance. It lights the way back to your center, helping you find balance even when the waves of anger, grief, or anxiety threaten to pull you under. Trust in its light—it will always guide you home.

Picture your emotions as the diverse crew members aboard your emotional vessel. Each one—whether it's joy, sadness, or anger—has a unique role to play. Emotional resilience isn't about silencing or dismissing these crew members but about fostering a healthy relationship with each. As their captain, you ensure they work together harmoniously to navigate the emotional seas.

Emotional resilience is more than a skill; it's an art form. Like a sculptor molding clay, you shape your emotional responses with intention and care. Each challenge becomes an opportunity to create something beautiful—a masterpiece that reflects your inner strength and adaptability.

In the vast sea of emotions, the siren song of self-compassion calls out, urging you to offer yourself kindness and understanding. Emotional resilience involves answering this call, recognizing that you are deserving of care and a safe harbor within yourself. Amidst life's storms, self-compassion becomes the anchor that grounds you in moments of uncertainty.

Mastering your emotional compass is a lifelong journey of self-discovery, growth, and artistry. With each storm navigated and each wave ridden, you refine your ability to steer through the chaos with grace. By embracing your emotions, shaping them with care, and anchoring yourself in self-compassion, you create a resilient symphony of inner strength—a masterpiece uniquely your own.

Key Takeaways

- **Navigate Your Emotions:** Use emotional resilience as a compass to find balance amidst life's highs and lows.
- **Adapt to Emotional Currents:** Emotions are fluid—learn to flow with them instead of resisting their natural ebb and flow.
- **Self-Compassion is Key:** Treat yourself with kindness, especially during emotional storms, to foster healing and growth.
- **Transform Challenges into Growth:** Use difficult emotions as opportunities for deeper understanding and strength.
- **Reflect and Reset:** Periodic reflection helps recalibrate your emotional compass, keeping you aligned with your well-being.

The Occasional Cosmic Curveball

Gather around, creative soul, because we're about to paint with the chaotic colors of existence. Life isn't about managing time like a dull taskmaster; it's about unleashing it on the canvas of your days, creating a vibrant, swirling masterpiece of deadlines, routines, and the occasional cosmic curveball. So, grab your brushes, dip them into the palette of priorities, and let's craft an extraordinary work of art called Your Life.

Picture your life as a blank canvas, stretched taut across the easel of the universe. Time is your paint—vivid, dynamic, and ready to be shaped by your vision. It's your canvas, your brush, your colors. No pressure, but each stroke is uniquely yours to make.

Time, like paint, isn't infinite. The tube has a finite supply of minutes, hours, and days. Each stroke counts. Wasting time is like pouring those precious hues down a drain, leaving your canvas blank. Treat your moments with intention—they're the building blocks of your masterpiece.

Life isn't a paint-by-numbers exercise. Your priorities are like Picasso's art—multifaceted, abstract, and sometimes delightfully chaotic. Don't be afraid to let your priorities overlap and dance on the canvas. It's in the chaos that your unique vision emerges.

Routine isn't the enemy; it's one of your most reliable brushes. Use it to lay down consistent patterns and strokes that form the backbone of your canvas. But beware—routine should be your tool, not your master. Stay intentional, and let it serve the masterpiece, not overshadow it.

Procrastination is the master illusionist in the gallery of time. It promises a grand reveal but rarely delivers. Like disappearing ink, it erases potential strokes before they're even made. Conquer it with discipline—the brush that ensures your ideas don't fade before they're realized.

Time can feel like Salvador Dalí's melting clocks—stretching, warping, and bending in ways that confuse and challenge. Instead of fighting it, dance with time's surrealism. Embrace its fluidity, twist it to your will, and ensure every distorted second adds to the vibrancy of your canvas.

Your palette isn't limited to black and white. Life is bursting with colors—experiences, challenges, and wild experiments. Splash your canvas with these vibrant hues, because monotony is the true thief of creativity. Each shade tells a story; let your canvas be alive with them.

Deadlines are the rhythmic drumbeats that keep your artistic process moving forward. They add structure, ensuring your masterpiece doesn't dissolve into chaos. Embrace them not as restrictions but as the pulse that drives your work to completion.

In a world cluttered with unnecessary details, sometimes the boldest statement is a minimalist one. Trim the excess from your canvas. Each stroke should be deliberate and impactful, conveying meaning without distraction. Simplicity, done right, can speak volumes.

Life isn't always about careful planning. Sometimes, it's the graffiti of spontaneity that gives your canvas character. Let unexpected splashes and rebellious strokes breathe life into your work. They're the surprises that add depth and authenticity to your masterpiece.

Time blocking is the jazz improvisation of productivity. Each block becomes an instrument, contributing to the rhythm of your day. Together, they form a harmonious composition that allows you to balance focus and flexibility while crafting your life's work.

Multitasking is a messy collage of half-finished strokes. True artistry lies in focusing on one stroke at a time. Give each task your full attention, and watch as your canvas transforms into a refined, cohesive masterpiece.

Distractions are the graffiti tags that obscure your canvas. They may seem colorful at first, but they dilute the beauty of your work. Be the vigilant curator of your time, removing distractions so your true vision can shine through.

Every great artist pauses to admire their work. Take moments to reflect on your progress. What worked? What didn't? Use the pen of self-awareness to jot notes in the margins of your canvas. Reflection is how you refine your process and grow as an artist.

Life isn't a single grand oil painting; it's a mosaic of small victories. Each tiny tile contributes to the larger picture. Celebrate these wins, for they're the vibrant pieces that bring your masterpiece to life.

Time vampires sneak in, splattering unwanted paint on your carefully crafted canvas. Identify these distractions, set boundaries, and guard your time like a curator protecting a priceless work of art. Your time is your masterpiece; treat it as such.

Life's splashes of unpredictability are like watercolor—flowing and blending in unexpected ways. Instead of resisting, adapt. Let the fluidity of these moments add depth and richness to your canvas. Flexibility is the brush that creates movement and life in your work.

Life occasionally splashes your canvas with unexpected ink blots. Instead of viewing them as mistakes, see them as opportunities. What can you create from them? Each ink blot has a hidden narrative, waiting to be revealed with patience and perspective.

Your canvas isn't two-dimensional; it's a living, breathing, multidimensional experience. Like wearing 3D glasses, broaden your perspective to see the layers and depth in your life's journey. Every challenge, success, and curveball adds richness to your work.

Your canvas is never truly complete. It's an ever-evolving masterpiece, a symphony of strokes, splashes, and stories that continues as long as you do. Embrace the unfinished nature of your work—it's what makes each new day a fresh opportunity to add to your legacy.

Carry your canvas with pride, and let the echoes of intentional strokes, spontaneous splatters, and the occasional cosmic curveball create a life that reflects your essence. This is your art, your story, your masterpiece. Keep painting.

Key Takeaways

- **Time is a Precious Resource:** Use your moments intentionally; every stroke on life's canvas adds to your masterpiece.
- **Balance Routine with Flexibility:** Routines provide structure, but adaptability ensures you thrive amid unexpected challenges.
- **Avoid the Illusion of Multitasking:** Focus on one task at a time for greater impact and fulfillment.
- **Reflect on Your Efforts:** Pause to assess what's working and what isn't, refining your approach as you move forward.
- **Celebrate Progress:** Life is a mosaic of small wins; appreciate each piece that contributes to the larger picture.

The Map to Liberation

Prepare to embark on a daring voyage into the uncharted waters of forgiveness. This is a journey where the heavy anchors of resentment are cast away, and the sails of liberation catch the winds of renewal. Forgiveness is more than an act—it's a treasure map guiding you toward the priceless riches of peace, freedom, and a lighter heart.

Picture resentment as a set of rusty anchors, dragging your ship through turbulent waters. Forgiveness isn't about polishing these weights; it's about cutting them loose. By releasing these burdens, you free your vessel to sail unencumbered into the open seas of possibility.

Forgiveness is your map to liberation—a compass pointing you toward the open waters of serenity. It doesn't ask you to forget the treacherous shores you've encountered but to chart a new course. With forgiveness as your guide, calmer horizons and brighter days lie ahead.

In the pirate's code, forgiveness is the ultimate treasure—not a sign of weakness but a declaration of strength. It's a bold and rebellious act, a choice to value freedom over the shackles of resentment. To forgive is to wield the sword of liberation and uncover the hidden treasures within.

Carrying grudges is like weighing your heart down with cannonballs of anger. Forgiveness is the tool that removes these weights, allowing your ship to rise and sail freely. Casting these burdens into the abyss isn't an act of surrender—it's an act of courage.

In life's vast ocean, harboring resentment is like sailing blindfolded through treacherous waters. Forgiveness removes the blindfold, offering clarity and direction. It's not a luxury but a necessity, a sextant that guides you to skies free of clouds and storms.

The mariner who forgives undergoes a profound transformation, shedding the barnacles of bitterness to emerge as a sleeker, swifter vessel. Forgiveness doesn't erase the past; it reclaims it, transforming scars into stories of resilience and growth.

Compassion becomes your guide as you navigate the vastness of human imperfection. Forgiveness isn't about excusing wrongdoing; it's about understanding that all ships encounter storms. Unfurl the sails of compassion and let them carry you toward empathy and peace.

In the world of forgiveness, the privateer seeks parley instead of plunder. Forgiveness isn't about defeating enemies; it's about transforming them into allies. Raise the flag of dialogue and engage with courage, fostering understanding instead of conflict.

Forgiveness requires vulnerability, like exposing your ship's underbelly to the unpredictable seas. It's not about being invincible but about embracing the authenticity of your humanity. In this vulnerability lies the strength to heal and grow.

Imagine forgiveness as a sea shanty—a melody that weaves through chapters of pain and redemption. It doesn't erase the verses of hardship but transforms them into a ballad of resilience. Sing your shanty boldly, letting its tune guide you toward healing.

To forgive is to offer clemency—not as a rescue mission for others, but as a release for yourself. It's about allowing those stranded on the islands of past grievances to build their own rafts, while you sail onward, unburdened and free.

In the act of forgiveness, you find a safe harbor—a place of solace in the stormy seas of emotion. Forgiveness doesn't erase the storms but helps you navigate them with a heart unburdened by anger or regret.

The captain who forgives wields a unique compass, one that doesn't point north but toward reconciliation. Forgiveness isn't about forgetting—it's about healing the wounds that mark your journey. It's a courageous voyage toward wholeness.

The true treasure of forgiveness is release—a liberation from the chains that bind your spirit. This treasure isn't found in external riches but in the discovery of inner peace. Unlock the chest of forgiveness and revel in the freedom it brings.

In forgiveness, rogue waves aren't threats but opportunities for reflection. These waves can be navigated with grace, transforming their power into momentum that carries you toward healing. Each wave becomes a testament to your resilience.

Forgiveness reflects not just your wounds but your resilience. It's not about hiding the scars but embracing them as evidence of your strength. Look into the maritime mirror and honor the story etched onto your hull.

Forgiveness hoists the jolly roger—not as a flag of conquest, but as a symbol of audacious resilience. It's a declaration that the storms within no longer hold power over you. By raising this flag, you embrace the freedom to sail unencumbered.

In the grand finale of forgiveness, avast your anchors with bold flair. Let the act of forgiveness be a statement—a declaration that your ship is ready to sail freely through life's vast seas. This isn't about timid release but a fearless embrace of freedom and renewal. Avast, courageous navigator, and set sail toward the open waters of liberation!

Key Takeaways
- **Let Go to Move Forward:** Forgiveness frees you from the anchors of resentment and opens the door to personal liberation.
- **Compassion is Key:** Understanding human imperfection fosters empathy and makes forgiveness possible.
- **Forgiveness Transforms:** It doesn't erase the past but turns wounds into lessons and growth.
- **Embrace Vulnerability:** Forgiving requires courage and openness, making it an act of strength, not weakness.
- **Discover Inner Peace:** True forgiveness is a gift you give yourself, releasing burdens and finding solace.

Back to the Garden

Welcome back to the Garden of Priorities, a sacred space where the flowers of balance bloom and the weeds of unnecessary chaos are pulled up by their roots. This isn't just about tending to your well-being—it's about cultivating a lush, vibrant life so intentional and beautiful that even Mother Nature would pause to take notes.

Life often feels like an overgrown jungle, with the vines of responsibilities choking out the sunlight of peace. The Garden of Priorities is your machete—the tool you use to clear the clutter and carve out serenity. Hack away at the excess and create a space where your well-being can thrive.

In this garden, you are the master gardener. The first task? Identify the weeds—the commitments and tasks that suffocate your joy. Pluck them out with purpose, leaving room for the flowers of passion and the trees of meaningful endeavors to flourish.

A thriving garden starts with healthy soil. In the Garden of Priorities, self-care is that nutrient-rich foundation. Without it, your well-being wilts like neglected blossoms. Water your garden regularly with practices that nurture your mental, emotional, and physical health, ensuring your priorities grow strong.

Boundaries are the sunlight that nourishes your garden. They allow your priorities to grow tall and vibrant, preventing the invasive shade of unnecessary demands. Cultivate robust boundaries with care, ensuring that your well-being basks in the warmth of intentional living.

Even the healthiest gardens need pruning. Clip away the branches of outdated obligations and commitments that no longer serve you. Pruning isn't a one-time act; it's a lifelong practice that ensures your garden stays orderly and nourishes what matters most.

Joy is the rarest and most precious orchid in your garden. It's not just a decorative flourish—it's the essence of a fulfilling life. Choose activities and pursuits that bring genuine happiness, and watch as your garden becomes vibrant with the colors of delight.

Healthy relationships are like orchards in your garden, yielding sweet, nourishing fruit. Invest time and care into bonds that matter, and let the laughter, support, and love of others enrich the soil of your well-being.

Regret and guilt are like compost—they may stink at first, but they break down into rich lessons that nurture growth. Use your past mistakes as fertilizer for resilience and wisdom. Transform what once weighed you down into nourishment for your flourishing priorities.

The roots of your garden are your core values, planted deep and anchoring every decision. When the storms of life rage, these roots keep you grounded. Revisit them regularly, nurture their growth, and let them guide your garden's expansion.

A thriving mind requires constant nourishment. In your Garden of Priorities, continuous learning is the greenhouse protecting you from the frost of stagnation. Keep the doors open, letting curiosity circulate and ensuring your mind stays fertile and growing.

Each mindful moment is a seed in your garden. Plant them generously, and watch as a forest of tranquility takes root. Mindfulness is the secret fertilizer that helps every moment contribute to the flourishing ecosystem of your well-being.

Gratitude is the fountain at the heart of your garden, refreshing and replenishing everything around it. Pause regularly to appreciate the beauty of your blooms, the strength of your roots, and the lessons learned from every season. Gratitude keeps your garden alive and thriving.

Every garden needs seasons of rest, and so do you. Allow the soil of your mind and body to rejuvenate during fallow periods. Rest is not weakness—it's preparation for the vibrant growth and flourishing blooms that lie ahead.

Be like the willow tree, swaying gracefully with the winds of change. Flexibility ensures that your well-being isn't uprooted by unexpected challenges. Adaptability is the key to maintaining balance in your carefully tended garden.

Stress is the twisting maze that threatens to entangle your priorities. Equip yourself with the shears of effective coping mechanisms, and snip your way through the tangles. Every labyrinth, no matter how complex, has an exit.

Sleep is the nourishing rain that drenches your garden each night. It replenishes your energy, nurtures your mental clarity, and ensures your priorities can grow strong. Never skimp on this essential ingredient for holistic well-being.

In a world obsessed with multitasking, single-tasking is the meditative act that allows you to focus on one bloom at a time. Give your full attention to each task or moment, and watch as your garden thrives under the care of your undivided presence.

Regularly harvest the fruits of reflection in your garden. What grew well this season? What didn't? Use these insights to refine your priorities and plan for the future. Reflection is the cyclical process that keeps your garden flourishing year after year.

The Garden of Priorities hums with its own melody—a symphony of balance, peace, and fulfillment. Listen closely to the rhythm of your heart, the harmony of your thoughts, and the cadence of your actions. When you're in tune, your entire garden will sing with the song of well-being.

The beauty of your Garden of Priorities is that it's always growing. With each deliberate choice, each moment of care, you plant the seeds of an ever-blooming future. As your garden flourishes, it becomes a reflection of intentional, joy-filled living.

So, master gardener, take up your tools and tend to your priorities with love and care. May your garden thrive, your well-being blossom, and your life become a radiant oasis of balance and purpose. Happy gardening!

Key Takeaways

- **Clear the Clutter:** The Garden of Priorities thrives when you remove unnecessary tasks and commitments, creating space for what truly matters.
- **Self-Care is Essential:** Prioritize your well-being as the nutrient-rich soil that nourishes all areas of your life.
- **Boundaries Shine Bright:** Healthy boundaries act like sunlight, empowering your priorities to grow while keeping out distractions.
- **Reflect and Refine:** Regularly assess your priorities and learn from each season of growth, using reflection to guide your next steps.
- **Flexibility Sustains Growth:** Adaptability, like the dance of a willow tree, ensures resilience amidst life's unexpected storms.
- **Gratitude Fuels Fulfillment:** Embrace gratitude as the fountain of your garden, refreshing your spirit and nurturing your joy.
- **Rest is Productive:** Allow time for rejuvenation; even a well-tended garden needs periods of rest to prepare for vibrant growth.
- **Focus is Power:** Single-tasking helps you give your full attention to each priority, ensuring your efforts are intentional and impactful.

Unlike Jellyfish Take Aim

We're not here to drift aimlessly like jellyfish, tossed around by the tides of circumstance. We're here to ride the waves with intention, steering our lives toward meaningful horizons. So, brace yourself for a journey that will challenge your comfort zone and inspire you to take control, one deliberate choice at a time.

Life is a vast, open ocean, teeming with endless possibilities. But without purpose, you risk becoming a lonely surfer caught in the riptide of mediocrity. Purposeful living is your surfboard, your guide through the swells, and it's time to catch the waves that matter most.

Driftwood floats aimlessly, carried by currents not of its choosing. Purposeful living, however, is the compass in your hand, pointing you toward your true direction. Without purpose, you're flotsam on the sea of societal expectations, lost in the tides of others' whims. Purpose gives you agency—it's your call to take the helm.

Drift sings a seductive tune, urging you to abandon effort and let the tides carry you where they will. But beware—drift is the cousin of regret, luring you toward a life of "what-ifs" and unfulfilled potential. Purposeful living is your earplugs, silencing the siren's song and keeping you focused on your journey.

Purpose is your North Star, a constant beacon in the cosmos of choices. Without it, you stumble through the wilderness of indecision. Purposeful living isn't just a star; it's the compass, map, and survival guide that illuminate the path ahead.

Comfortable drift is a silent assassin, lulling you into stagnation with whispers of ease and familiarity. Purposeful living disrupts this false comfort. It's the alarm clock that jolts you awake, reminding you of the dreams waiting to be chased.

Imagine your life as a ship adrift on the sea. Without purpose, the winds and waves dictate your direction. Purposeful living places a steady captain at the helm, steering with clarity and determination through storms, calm seas, and every wave in between.

Drifters collect the dust of missed opportunities, the residue of unfulfilled potential. Purposeful living is your duster, sweeping away hesitation, clearing procrastination, and leaving a clean slate for deliberate action.

Drift is a shimmering mirage, promising ease but delivering emptiness. Purposeful living is the true oasis, offering fulfillment, direction, and the motivation to keep moving forward through the sands of uncertainty.

Purposeful living is an act of rebellion—a defiant stand against conformity and mediocrity. While drifters march in line, blending into the monotony, those with purpose blaze their own trail. It's a battle cry, a declaration that your life will be lived boldly and intentionally.

Drifters leave no footprints, their lives unnoticed in the sands of time. Purposeful living is your heavy boots, leaving a trail that shouts, "I was here, and I mattered." It's about creating a legacy, one deliberate step at a time.

Life without purpose is like a silent movie—flat and unremarkable. Purposeful living provides the soundtrack, a symphony of energy, rhythm, and joy that keeps you moving forward with passion.

Drift is a whirlpool of false promises, pulling you into the abyss of regret. Purposeful living is your buoy, keeping you afloat and steering you toward meaningful choices and a life without "what-ifs."

Drift creates accidental splatters, random strokes with no intention or design. Purposeful living is your brushstroke, bold and deliberate, painting a masterpiece that tells your unique story.

Drifters are unwritten novels, stuck in a never-ending prologue. Purposeful living is your epic saga, filled with plot twists, triumphs, and chapters of growth. It's the kind of story that captivates, inspires, and leaves a lasting impression.

Life is a stormy sea, and purpose is the lighthouse that guides you through the turbulence. Drifters are sailors lost in the tempest, yearning for direction. Purposeful living is the beacon that keeps you steady, even when the waves crash hard.

Imagine life as a construction site. Drifters lack the tools to build anything meaningful, leaving behind collapsed structures and unfinished dreams. Purposeful living is your toolbox, equipping you with everything you need to construct a life that stands tall and proud.

Drift is discordant noise, a jumble of missed chances and wasted time. Purposeful living is a symphony—each note intentional, each movement a step closer to the crescendo of a life lived with meaning.

Purposeful living is not a passive act. It's a series of deliberate choices, bold brushstrokes, and powerful declarations. Avoid the tempting allure of drift and take the helm with conviction. You are the captain of your ship, and purposeful living is your compass in this grand adventure. Ride the waves, steer through the storms, and create a life that resonates with meaning, fulfillment, and the undeniable mark of your unique existence.

Key Takeaways
- **Purpose is Your Compass:** A clear sense of purpose steers you through life's uncertainties and keeps you grounded.
- **Avoid Comfortable Drift:** Stagnation may feel safe but leads to regret—challenge yourself to pursue growth.
- **Create Your Legacy:** Live boldly, leaving footprints and a trail of meaningful contributions behind you.
- **Intentional Living is a Rebellion:** Reject mediocrity and conformity by pursuing a life aligned with your values and dreams.
- **Celebrate Your Story:** Purposeful living turns your life into an epic saga, filled with deliberate choices and unforgettable moments.

Life's Balancing Act

Ready yourself for a cosmic voyage into the mysterious realm of time management, where the seconds are the stars guiding your ship through the vast expanse of goals, priorities, and all the other celestial stuff. This ain't your average dance; it's the time tango, a symphony of chaos and order, with you as the fearless conductor.

Imagine time as the cosmic clockwork, a grand mechanism ticking away with relentless precision. But fear not, for in this celestial dance, you're not a mere spectator; you're the choreographer of your destiny, orchestrating the ballet of goals, priorities, and the whole cosmic shebang.

Goals, those elusive sirens, beckon with promises of treasure at the end of the rainbow. But beware, for not all treasures are worth the pursuit. In the time tango, discernment is your compass, guiding you to goals that harmonize with your soul's melody.

Priorities, the partners in your time tango, waltz in and out with a grace that demands attention. The art lies in mastering the priority polka, where each step is deliberate, ensuring that the dance floor of your life remains uncluttered and harmonious.

Life's a juggling act, a vivacious jive where responsibilities, passions, and the unexpected are the colorful balls in the air. The trick is not to drop the balls but to dance with them in rhythm, a jester in the court of time, entertaining chaos with grace.

As a time traveler in the time tango, dilemmas abound like portals to alternate realities. Choosing between what's urgent and what's important requires a discerning eye. The time traveler's dilemma is not about speed but about direction.

The cosmic choreography of time management is not a rigid routine but a spontaneous dance where goals and priorities pirouette across the stage of your existence. It's not about sticking to the script; it's about embracing the improvised brilliance of the moment.

Schedules are the instruments in the symphony of time, each playing a unique note. In the time tango, the symphony isn't about perfection but about creating a melody that resonates with the rhythm of your heart. Adjust the tempo, change the key, and let the symphony play on.

In the time tango, the magician's secret lies in the art of time warping. It's not about bending time to your will but about making time an ally. With a wave of your wand, transform the mundane into the magical, and let the time warp commence.

Goals are the unexplored horizons on the map of your journey. As an explorer of time, chart your course with audacious curiosity.

Navigate not just towards the visible goals but also towards the hidden gems that shimmer on the edges of your perception.

Balancing goals and priorities is a tightrope walk in the circus of life. The trick is not just to stay on the tightrope but to dance on it with flair. Each step is a choice, a delicate pirouette between the gravity of obligations and the weightlessness of dreams.

A navigator in the time tango relies on a unique compass—purpose. Goals and priorities find their true north in the compass of purpose. As you navigate through the cosmic currents, let purpose be the guiding star that keeps your ship true.

Goals are the seeds, priorities are the watering cans, and time is the fertile soil. The gardener of time management doesn't just plant; they cultivate and harvest. Witness the blossoming of your efforts and savor the fruits of your well-tended temporal garden.

In the time tango, adopt the stargazer's perspective. Goals are the constellations guiding your journey, priorities are the planets aligning in your favor. Connect the dots, read the celestial signs, and navigate the vastness with the wisdom of an interstellar traveler.

Goals and priorities are the puppeteer's strings in the cosmic marionette show of life. But here, you're not a puppet; you're the puppeteer. Master the art of pulling the strings with intention, creating a dance that reflects your authenticity.

Time is the alchemist's crucible, where goals and priorities undergo transmutation. It's not about turning lead into gold but about transforming moments into memories, dreams into reality. Embrace the alchemy of time, and let each second be a drop in the elixir of your existence.

Balancing goals and priorities is an acrobatic feat, a dance on the narrow beam of existence. The acrobat doesn't fear the heights; they relish the challenge. In the time tango, become the virtuoso acrobat, executing flips of creativity and somersaults of focus.

Goals and priorities are the raw marble in the sculptor's hands. Carve with purpose, and let the sculpture of your life emerge with each intentional stroke. The sculptor doesn't rush; they savor the process, revealing the masterpiece within the uncut stone.

Listen to the whispers of time, for it holds secrets untold. The time whisperer deciphers these secrets, understanding that not every ticking second is the same. In the time tango, attune your ears to the subtle rhythms, and let time reveal its enigmatic dance.

Adopt the Magellan mindset in your time voyage. Goals are the uncharted territories, and priorities are the maps. Embrace the spirit of exploration, face the storms with resilience, and let the Magellan in you navigate the seas of time.

As a voyager in the grand time tango, pledge an oath to the cosmic clock. Let your oath be a declaration of intention, a promise to dance with purpose, and a commitment to savor every step in the intricate dance of goals, priorities, and all the other celestial stuff.

Remember, the most harmonious melodies are those that resonate deeply with the essence of who we are. The power of choice lies within your hands—or more aptly, within your heart. Not every note, technique, or method will align with the rhythm of your soul. And that's more than okay—it's expected. The beauty of this journey lies in the freedom to choose what works for you and gracefully set aside what doesn't. It's about crafting a personal symphony that reflects the depth, complexity, and uniqueness of your being.

Reflections for the Journey

Before you step out of "Orchestrating Impact: Conducting Life's Symphony with Purpose and Resilience" and into Life's Balancing Act, remember these reflections. They're the guiding lights in the concert hall of life, illuminating the path to a symphony that's uniquely yours—played with passion, conducted with purpose, and echoed with resilience.

1. **The Symphony of Now** In the eternal dance of life, every moment pulses with music. Embrace the 'now' as your symphony plays, for it's in these fleeting beats that the essence of existence sings.
2. **Authenticity's Melody** Let the music within you play freely, unencumbered by the world's noise. Your authenticity is your melody, a unique rhythm that defines the dance of your life.
3. **Courageous Crescendos** Face life's challenges with the courage of a maestro facing a tumultuous orchestra. Each decision, a bold crescendo, amplifies your strength, echoing courage through the symphony of your existence.
4. **Resilience's Rhythm** When adversity strikes, let resilience be your rhythm, keeping time in the face of discord. It's the beat that sustains you, ensuring the music never stops.
5. **The Harmony of Self-Compassion** In the composition of life, self-compassion harmonizes the notes. It's a soothing melody that heals and nurtures, allowing you to play on with grace and strength.

6. **Flexibility's Flow**   Like a river's meander, flexibility in life's symphony ensures the music flows, uninterrupted by the rocks of rigidity. Adapt and improvise, for in flexibility, there's beauty.

7. **Tenacity's Tempo**   Let tenacity set your tempo, a steadfast beat against the storm. It's the persistent drum that resonates with determination, driving the symphony forward.

8. **Introspection's Interlude**   In the quiet spaces between life's movements, introspection offers a reflective pause. These interludes are essential, allowing you to tune into your inner symphony with clarity and purpose.

9. **Acceptance's Accord**   In life's symphony, acceptance is the chord that brings harmony. It's the understanding that all notes, whether joyful or somber, contribute to the beauty of the whole.

10. **The Conductor's Baton of Personal Power**   You wield the baton of personal power, guiding the symphony within. Direct your life's music with intention, blending the notes into a masterpiece of your making.

11. **The Sonata of Individuality:** Celebrate the sonata of your individuality, a composition that resonates with the authenticity of your being. Each key struck is a declaration of your unique presence in the world's orchestra.

12. **Lifelong Learning's Legacy**   The symphony within is enriched with each lesson learned. Lifelong learning is the melody that evolves, a testament to your growth and the endless beauty of your internal composition.

Building the Relational Tapestry

Across these chapters, a unified theme emerges: the journey toward cultivating rich, fulfilling relationships is both intricate and essential. We're guided to weave our tapestry with intention, exploring the depths of genuine connections, and courageously unbinding ourselves from the chains of unhealthy ties. Each chapter offers unique insights and actionable steps to enrich our relational tapestry. As we draw these discussions to a close, our final reflections converge on some pivotal lessons, underscoring the journey's core insights and offering a pathway to enrich our interconnected web of life.

1. **Inventory and Reflection**   Regularly assess the state of your relationships, acknowledging the beauty in each connection and identifying areas for growth or release.
2. **Cultivate Authenticity**   Be genuine in your interactions, embracing vulnerability as a strength and fostering an environment where authenticity is celebrated.
3. **Practice Active Listening and Empathy**   Deepen your connections through active listening and empathy, ensuring every thread in your tapestry feels seen, heard, and valued.
4. **Set and Respect Boundaries**   Establish clear boundaries to protect your emotional well-being and respect those of others, fostering healthy, balanced relationships.
5. **Embrace Diversity and Change**   Welcome the diverse threads that each person weaves into your life, and remain open to the growth and change that each relationship brings.
6. **Invest in Emotional Intelligence**   Enhance your relationships through emotional intelligence, understanding and managing your emotions and those of others for deeper connections.
7. **Nurture Shared Experiences**   Create and cherish shared moments and experiences, as these are the stitches that strengthen the fabric of your relationships.

8. **Let Go of What No Longer Serves You** Courageously release connections that hinder your growth, making room for new threads that enrich your tapestry.

By integrating these lessons, we embark on a transformative journey toward a richer, more vibrant relational life. As we weave, untangle, and sometimes re-weave the threads of our connections, we create a living tapestry that reflects the depth, complexity, and beauty of human relationships.

Nurturing Your True Self

Across these chapters, a unified theme emerges: the journey to authenticity demands more than just the desire to peel away society's expectations; it requires actionable steps, reflective practices, and a steadfast commitment to nurturing our true selves. Herein lies a strategic blueprint to navigate the terrain of dispelling illusions and wholeheartedly welcoming your authentic self. This guide serves as your compass, offering direction and strategies to embark on this transformative journey, ensuring each step taken is grounded in purpose, reflection, and an enduring commitment to unveiling and celebrating the true you. As we draw these discussions to a close, our final reflections converge on some pivotal lessons, underscoring the journey's core insights and offering a pathway to enrich our interconnected web of life.

1. **Audit Your Cares Budget** Take inventory of where your cares are currently invested. List out the things, people, and pursuits you're dedicating your emotional currency to. Then, critically assess each one: Does it reflect your true values, or is it a product of societal expectation?

Redirect your emotional investment towards what genuinely matters to you.

2. **Cultivate Self-Discovery**   Engage in activities that foster self-discovery. Journaling, meditation, and solo travel are potent tools for unearthing your authentic desires and aspirations. Set aside dedicated time each week to explore your inner landscape, seeking to understand the melody of your soul.

3. **Continue the Practice of Saying No**   Strengthen your ability to say no to things that don't align with your authentic self. Start small, perhaps by declining invitations or requests that don't resonate with you. Each act of saying no is a step towards reclaiming your time and energy for the things that truly matter.

4. **Embrace Vulnerability**   Authenticity and vulnerability go hand in hand. Begin sharing more of your true thoughts and feelings with others, even when it feels uncomfortable. Start with trusted friends or family, gradually expanding your circle as you become more confident in your authentic expression.

5. **Deconstruct Societal Masks**   Identify the roles and masks you wear that are more about societal approval than genuine self-expression. For each mask, ask yourself why you put it on and what fears are associated with taking it off. Begin experimenting with removing these masks in safe environments.

6. **Curate Your Influence**   Assess the sources of influence in your life—social media, peer groups, family expectations. Consciously curate these influences, distancing yourself from those that reinforce the illusion and drawing closer to those that encourage authenticity.

7. **Celebrate Your Uniqueness**   Identify traits, interests, and aspirations that make you unique, and find ways to

celebrate and express them daily. Whether through your style, hobbies, or work, let these unique aspects shine.

8. **Reflect and Adjust**   Regularly reflect on your journey towards authenticity. What felt liberating? What challenges did you encounter? Use these reflections to adjust your course, fine-tuning your approach to align more closely with your true self.

Activities for Embracing Authenticity:

- **Authenticity Journal**   Keep a journal dedicated to your journey of authenticity. Use it to record insights, challenges, and victories along the way.
- **No Week Challenge**   Dedicate a week to practicing saying no to things that don't align with your authentic self. Reflect on the experience.
- **Unmasking Ritual**   Create a personal ritual for letting go of societal masks. This could involve a physical activity, like a symbolic burning of written fears or expectations, or a quiet meditation focused on releasing these burdens.
- **Authentic Expression Project**   Start a project that allows you to express your unique self, such as writing, art, or creating a personal blog or vlog. Let this project be a testament to your individuality and a celebration of your authentic expression.

By following this roadmap and engaging with these activities, you're not just unmasking the illusion—you're stepping into a symphony of authenticity, composed by and for you. Your authentic self is the most beautiful and resonant note. Play it loud, play it proud, and let the world hear the true melody of who you are.

When you are ready for more, consider these steps for orchestrating your inner symphony:

1. **Conduct Your Day**   Start each morning by setting an intention that aligns with your inner symphony. Consider what melody you wish to play today—perhaps it's courage, resilience, or joy. Let this intention guide your actions and interactions throughout the day.

2. **Tune Out the Noise**   Dedicate a period each day to disconnect from external pressures. This could be through digital detoxes, quiet walks, or simply sitting in silence. Use this time to listen to the quieter notes of your inner melody.

3. **Self-Discovery Overture**   Journal about the different facets of your identity as if they were instruments in your symphony. What unique sound does each one contribute? How do they harmonize to create the music of 'you'?

4. **Authenticity Crescendo**   Identify moments when you feel most authentic and alive. What are you doing? Who are you with? Reflect on how you can amplify these moments in your life to let your true self play louder.

5. **Resilience Strings**   Reflect on a recent challenge and how you navigated it. Write about the 'music' you used to endure—was it a slow, steady tune or a powerful anthem? Celebrate your resilience and consider how it enriches your symphony.

6. **Bold Brass Moments**   Think of a time when you needed to stand up for yourself or make your presence known. How did you summon the courage? Create a 'bold brass' playlist that inspires you to amplify your convictions.

7. **Woodwind Flexibility**   Practice flexibility by introducing small changes into your routine. Notice how adaptation feels and journal about the experience. Is it uncomfortable, liberating, or both?

8. **Percussion of Tenacity**   Set a challenging goal for yourself, something that requires persistence. Break it

down into actionable steps and track your progress, celebrating each 'beat' of achievement.

9. **Choir of Compassion**   Perform a daily act of self-kindness. This could be forgiving a mistake, treating yourself, or simply offering words of encouragement. Note how these acts influence the harmony of your inner symphony.

10. **Solo of Introspection**   Spend time in solitude reflecting on your values, dreams, and the music you want to make in the world. Consider how your actions contribute to or detract from this vision.

11. **Symphony of Connection**   Reach out to someone who adds beautiful harmony to your life. Share your appreciation for their presence and explore how you can create more beautiful music together.

12. **Lifelong Learning Cadence**   Commit to learning something new that resonates with your inner symphony. This could be a skill, hobby, or area of knowledge. Reflect on how this new learning enriches your music.

13. **Silence Between the Notes**   Incorporate moments of silence into your daily life to appreciate the music you're creating. Use these pauses to breathe, reflect, and prepare for the next note.

14. **Reflective Encore**   At the end of each week, reflect on the music you've created. What felt harmonious? What notes would you change? Use these reflections to fine-tune your symphony moving forward.

Congratulations, you've not only mastered the time tango but also conducted a symphony of purpose and audacity. May your steps be filled with purpose, your rhythms be harmonious, and your dance be an everlasting celebration of existence.

Afterword for the Book

As we reach the end of this journey through the intricate landscape of self-discovery and intentional living, my heart is full of gratitude for having you here, alongside me. I hope these reflections, insights, and practices have sparked a desire within you to build a life guided by purpose, not by the pull of distractions. This book was never meant to hand you all the answers but to be a companion in the ongoing process of sculpting a life that feels truly yours.

Remember, this isn't a solitary adventure but a dance we all share, each of us adding our unique rhythm. Your distinctiveness, your quirks, and the inner vision you hold—these are the very essence of a life that leaves an imprint on the world. As you move forward, lean into your path with confidence, embrace the unknown with a sense of curiosity, and let your choices inspire others to seek their own version of fulfillment.

May you lead with a compassionate heart, an open mind, and a commitment to living in alignment with your highest values. And in those moments where you feel uncertain or discouraged, know that the life you are shaping is a testament to the intentional choices you make. This isn't a goodbye; it's a standing invitation to keep stepping forward with purpose. Because at the end of the day, it's not about a life perfectly planned—it's about one crafted with care, with thought, and with love.

To a life well-lived and deeply felt.

With gratitude and respect,

William R. Stanek

About the Author: William R. Stanek

Meet the Visionary, the Storyteller, and Your Guide on the Journey to Intentional Living

Biography

William R. Stanek is no ordinary author in the world of personal growth. With a background that's woven with more experiences than can be counted, Stanek is known for his straightforward wisdom, practical insights, and a talent for helping others build lives that align with their core values. His work speaks to those who seek authenticity and a real connection to their purpose, bringing an inspiring yet realistic approach to the journey of self-discovery.

Throughout his journey, Stanek has played many roles—teacher, innovator, mentor, and artist—each experience adding to the perspective he shares in his books. He is known for being the voice people turn to when conventional advice falls short and when what's needed isn't a quick fix but a path to meaningful change. Over his career, he has helped countless individuals rethink their relationship with success, personal growth, and what it truly means to live a purposeful life.

As a leader and technologist at the intersection of business, technology, and leadership, William's work extends far beyond the written word. He has spent years inspiring action, driving meaningful change, and guiding others on how to create impact that resonates, endures, and honors each individual's unique journey. His influence spans professions and walks of life, providing a grounding perspective in a world that often encourages us to chase everything at once. In this book, William shares his experiences, insights, and deep conviction in the power of intentional living with a broader audience.

Connect with William R. Stanek

Join William in exploring new ideas, challenging conventional wisdom, and pushing the boundaries of what's possible in personal growth. Connect with him here:

LinkedIn: Follow William for updates, articles, and perspectives on intentional living and personal growth.

https://www.linkedin.com/in/williamstanek/

Facebook: Like his author page for daily insights, reflections, and updates.

http://www.facebook.com/William.Stanek.Author

Twitter: Follow for thought-provoking tweets and personal growth tips in 280 characters.

http://www.twitter.com/WilliamStanek

Website: Visit http://www.williamrstanek.com to learn more about his books, workshops, and other projects.

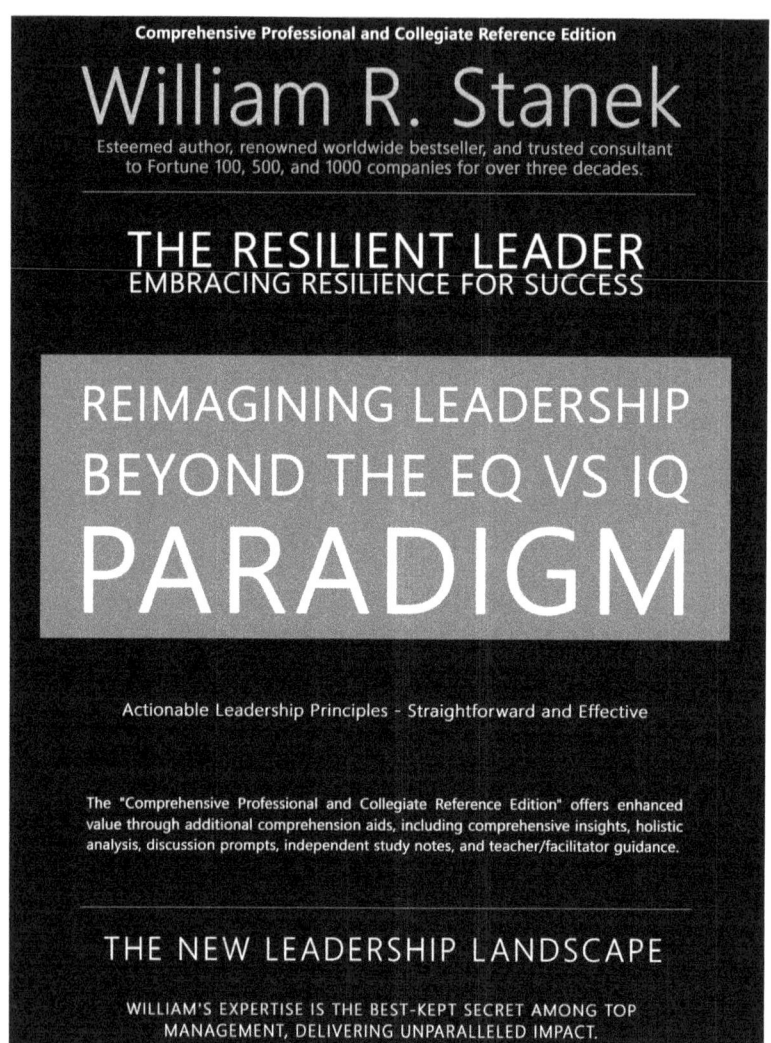

"The Resilient Leader, Embracing Resilience for Success" stands out in the crowded landscape of leadership and emotional intelligence books by offering a fresh, holistic approach to leadership that transcends traditional models. This groundbreaking work by William R. Stanek redefines the essence of effective leadership in the modern era, distinguishing itself through several key differentiators:

- **Holistic Integration of Multiple Intelligences**   While most leadership books focus on emotional intelligence (EQ) or traditional cognitive intelligence (IQ), "The Resilient Leader, Embracing Resilience for Success" introduces readers to the 8 Pillars of Leadership. This innovative framework encompasses Emotional Resilience, Creative Intelligence, Practical Intelligence, Cultural Intelligence, Intrapersonal Intelligence, Interpersonal Intelligence, Ethical Intelligence, and Analytical Intelligence. By embracing a broader spectrum of intelligences, the book equips leaders with a multifaceted toolkit, enabling them to navigate the complexities of the contemporary landscape more effectively than ever before.

- **Emphasis on Emotional Resilience**   "The Resilient Leader, Embracing Resilience for Success" delves deep into emotional resilience, offering readers actionable strategies to cultivate this essential trait. The book presents emotional resilience as the bedrock of leadership excellence, enabling leaders to withstand challenges, adapt to change, thrive in adversity, and so much more. Whereas most literature on emotional intelligence or emotional resilience treats resilience as a narrow set of traits or a subset of emotional intelligence, "The Resilient Leader, Embracing Resilience for Success" reconceptualizes it as a multifaceted intelligence in its own right. This book goes far beyond the typical definitions and presents emotional resilience as a complex, dynamic intelligence that is critical for effective leadership.

- **Rigorous Self-Assessment Tool**   Distinct from other leadership books that offer generalized advice, "The Resilient Leader, Embracing Resilience for Success" integrates a cutting-edge self-assessment tool. This personalized assessment allows readers to evaluate their strengths and areas for growth, providing a tailored roadmap for personal and professional development. This actionable, data-driven approach ensures that readers can make concrete progress on their leadership journey.

- **Case Studies and Real-World Application** While many books on leadership and emotional intelligence rely on theoretical principles, "The Resilient Leader, Embracing Resilience for Success" grounds its insights in practical reality. Through a series of detailed case studies featuring real-world scenarios and leadership challenges, the book illustrates how the principles of resilient leadership can be applied in various contexts. From crisis management in the financial sector to navigating complex mergers and leading through global pandemics, these case studies offer readers a window into the transformative power of resilient leadership in action.

- **Future-Oriented Leadership Vision** Stanek's book critically examines the evolution of leadership theories and practices, from ancient times through the industrial revolution to the present day, offering a visionary outlook on the future of leadership. Unlike books that dwell on past or current leadership models, "The Resilient Leader, Embracing Resilience for Success" charts a course for the future, advocating for a comprehensive, adaptable leadership approach that meets the demands of an ever-changing world. This forward-thinking perspective encourages leaders to not only adapt to the new normal but to thrive within it, paving the way for a new era of leadership excellence.

In summary, "The Resilient Leader, Embracing Resilience for Success" offers a unique, comprehensive guide that goes beyond traditional leadership tenets, providing readers with the insights and tools needed to excel in today's dynamic environment. By combining a holistic view of intelligence, a focus on emotional resilience, practical tools for self-assessment, real-world applicability, and a visionary leadership approach, this book is an essential resource for anyone looking to lead effectively in the 21st century.

www.ingramcontent.com/pod-product-compliance
Lightning Source LLC
Chambersburg PA
CBHW071855160426
43209CB00005B/1063